THE WIT:

As with other married folks, money quarrels topped the list of disputes between the First Couple. Once, fuming about the bills from couturiers, specialty shops, and department stores, which approached $150,000 in a single year, Jack said, "She's unbelievable. She thinks she can go on spending forever. I don't understand what the hell she's doing with all those things. God, she's driving me crazy, absolutely crazy."

But Jackie wouldn't curtail her shopping sprees and the bills kept coming in. Looking over them one month, Kennedy turned to an aide and asked ruefully, "Is there a Spender's Anonymous?"

THE CHARM:

Kennedy's schedule was so overloaded that, inevitably, he missed some appointments. But, as he did at home when he was a child and as a preppie, he would charm his way out of trouble. "Everyone forgives him," said a close friend. "He gives them that big ingenuous grin, when actually he's about as ingenuous as an I.B.M. machine."

THE TEARS:

In November, 1963, Kennedy, reading the Texas newspapers, decided that something had to be done to heal the schism there between two opposing factions of the Democratic Party. With 1964 not far off, Kennedy would not take any chances with almost 10 percent of the Electoral College votes he would need for reelection. He decided to go to Texas to heal the rift.

It was not a journey he would willingly undertake.

JFK-

*The Wit,
The Charm, The Tears:
Remembrances from
Camelot*

LESTER DAVID AND IRENE DAVID

PaperJacks LTD.

TORONTO   NEW YORK

AN ORIGINAL

PaperJacks

JFK—THE WIT, THE CHARM, THE TEARS:
REMEMBRANCES FROM CAMELOT

PaperJacks LTD.

330 STEELCASE RD. E., MARKHAM, ONT. L3R 2M1
210 FIFTH AVE., NEW YORK, N.Y. 10010

First edition November 1988

10 9 8 7 6 5 4 3 2 1

ISBN 0-7701-0938-1

. . . Bright was your eye,
O! Why did you leave us, Eoghan? Why did you
die?

— Thomas Davis,
*Lament for the Death
of Eoghan Ruadh O'Neill*

Life is unfair.

— John F. Kennedy

For Alexander Michael and Sarah Nan
And the others who may yet come.

Contents

JFK

The Wit,
The Charm, The Tears:
Remembrances from
Camelot

A Kind of Prologue

Even in maturity, he had not lost the boyish look. There was the wide grin, the rebellious cowlick in the reddish-brown hair, the crinkles at the corners of his eyes, the sense of fun he could never repress for long. Because of this, because of his energy, his style, and his cool, he held an almost mystic appeal for the young. "He was a friend, our hope, a member of the family. He was like . . . a bigger brother," the students of the West Kinney Junior High School in Newark, New Jersey, wrote in their newspaper when they heard what happened in Dallas.

Little wonder, for he was young himself, only forty-three when he was elected President, and twenty-seven years younger than his predecessor in the Oval Office. He had a galvanic effect on all Americans who responded to the verve, freshness, and, yes, the glamour of the new First Family, a change from the eight relatively calm, but essentially boring years of the administration of Dwight D. Eisenhower.

Not all of the 1,035 days he served as the nation's thirty-fifth President were good ones. Some were dreadful, indeed. The disaster at the Bay of Pigs was one of the worst incidents in United States history. The showdown with Russia over the missiles in Cuba brought the world to the crumbling edge of nuclear devastation. He presided over a sharp escalation in the war with Vietnam, helping to ensnare the country into the unwinnable conflict.

Balancing these elements were the prideful accomplishments. He gave the civil rights movement a mighty thrust forward. A treaty banning the testing of nuclear weapons in the atmosphere, outer space, and underwater was ratified and signed by the United States, Great Britain, and Russia. He initiated a space program that ultimately landed an American on the moon.

John Kennedy's personal life was hardly beyond reproach. He liked women and enjoyed many of them, before he was elected President and after, before he was married and after. At the same time, he was a devoted family man whose two children became America's darlings. There were, too, family tragedies: the illness of his father, the death of a newborn baby.

All of this is chronicled in this book, although not in the usual way.

The life of John Kennedy, the crucible that formed his character and personality, the school

2

years, the war years, the dazzling woman he married — all are told through the medium of intimate, up-close, behind-the-scenes anecdotes that reveal, as little else could, the man and his work.

The reader will find that each major segment of John Kennedy's life is preceded by a brief factual account of what occurred during that period.

Kennedy once said, "I look forward to a world which will be safe not only for democracy and diversity, but also for personal distinction."

Through many stories from all phases of his life and career, this book seeks to show that John Fitzgerald Kennedy himself possessed that quality of personal distinction to a rare degree.

Road to the White House

Part One

Road to the White House

Chapter One

Schoolboy

John Kennedy's great-grandfathers arrived on Noddles Island in Boston Harbor in 1845 and 1848, jammed into steerage compartments of packet ships they had boarded at the port city of New Ross in Ireland's County Wexford. They were among the hordes fleeing the devastating potato famine and typhus epidemic that took hundreds of thousands of lives before the mid-century.

The paths of Thomas Fitzgerald and Patrick Kennedy never crossed, neither in Ireland nor America, but they were the forebears of two of the most famous and surely the liveliest political families in our nation's history, one branch of which produced a President.

Patrick, whose first job was as a barrel maker, married Bridget Murphy and raised four children. Their only son, Patrick J., was a brawny lad who worked on the Boston docks but quickly rose in station to own two saloons. Friendly and intelligent, he moved easily into

*politics and eventually served five terms in the Massa-
chusetts state legislature.*

*Tom, who married Rose Mary Murray, had eleven
children, one of whom was John F. "Honey Fitz" Fitzgerald, who became mayor of Boston and the man John
F. Kennedy called his political as well as familial ances-
tor. Honey Fitz was elected three times to Congress and
twice as mayor.*

*Honey Fitz's black-haired, blue-eyed daughter Rose
married Pat's gangling son, Joseph Patrick, on October
7, 1914. Joe and Rose had nine children in seventeen
years; the second, John Fitzgerald Kennedy, was born
on May 29, 1917, in a three-story gray frame house at 83
Beals Street in Boston's Brookline section. From his earliest days, the family called him Jack.*

*By the mid-1920s, Joe Kennedy was many times a
millionaire from stock market, motion picture, and real
estate investments. But rich as he was, he was not accepted by the elite families in Boston, the intellectually
and socially cultivated Brahmin. When his application
for membership in the prestigious Cohasset Country
Club was denied, Joe exploded. "Boston," he raged, "is
no place to bring up Irish children."*

*And so he moved away. He rented a private railroad
car and transported his family to Riverdale, an exclusive section in northwest New York City, closer to his
financial interests and where he hoped his family would
not face anti-Catholic bias. A few years later, Kennedy
moved his family to the exclusive suburb of Bronxville,
New York, and purchased a home at Hyannis Port on
Cape Cod. Winters were spent at Palm beach.*

*Jack's education had begun at the Dexter School in
Brookline. In New York, he went from the fourth
through sixth grades at Riverdale Country Day School,*

where teachers remember him as a serious student with a special aptitude for history and a dismal record in English. When he entered his teen years, he was enrolled by Joe in Canterbury School, in New Milford, Connecticut, a Catholic institution where he remained but a brief time.

In his dormitory just before Easter, he was awakened by a severe pain in his groin. It was diagnosed as acute appendicitis and he underwent surgery. When his convalescence was over, Jack accompanied his family to Hyannis Port and did not return to Canterbury.

That fall, Joe Kennedy decided Jack should follow his older brother to the Choate Preparatory School in Wallingford, Connecticut. Choate's 150-acre campus was typical of a New England school, its academic and social outlook similar to that of an English public school, notably Eton. The student body was largely Protestant. Among the graduates when Jack entered in 1931 were Adlai Stevenson and Chester Bowles, both of whom would play prominent roles in his administration.

During his first two years at Choate, Jack lived in the shadow of his brother Joe, two years older, who starred on the football and baseball fields, rowed on the crew team, was a brilliant student, and easily the most popular youth on campus. After Joe went on to Harvard, Jack's academic record did not improve. To the dismay of the school administration, he developed into a troublemaker. He and his misbehaving pals were labeled "public enemies" by the headmaster.

In his last two years at Choate, he roomed with K. Lemoyne Billings, a doctor's son who became his lifelong friend and a kind of gofer and confidant of the family, including its younger members. Lem Billings died in 1981.

Jack Kennedy graduated from Choate in 1935, the sixty-fifth in a class of one hundred ten, and followed Joe to Harvard.

Joe's No. 2 Son

In 1928, Joe paid $25,000 for a large white three-gabled house that sat on a bluff overlooking Nantucket Sound at Hyannis Port. Then known as the "Malcom Place," he converted it into a fifteen-room, nine-bath home and, without realizing it at the time, established the residence of the famous Kennedy compound. Ultimately, smaller homes for Jack, Bobby, and Eunice and Sargent Shriver would be built on the two and one-half acres. Ted and Joan would purchase a ten-room house a mile and a half away on Squaw Island. The compound became a prime tourist attraction, and sight-seeing launches would cruise the sound, packed with visitors eager to catch glimpses of the Kennedys at play.

But in the twenties and early thirties, no sightseers came. The nine Kennedy children and their friends romped all day long during summers and vacations on the sloping lawn and the beach, but it was not free play. Joe was as rigid about their playtime as he was about his business dealings.

Before going to sleep, the Kennedy kids would consult the next day's schedule which was posted on the broad porch of the Big House, as it came to be known. Wake-up time was seven A.M. Then all of them went out on the lawn for sitting-up exercises. At eight sharp, inside for breakfast, a large one: juice, eggs, hot cereal, and gallons of milk. Twenty minutes later, everyone was to be out on the athletic fields.

The schedule called for an hour of tennis, followed by an hour of basketball, and another of touch football or softball. Then came a cooling-off period and, at one-thirty, a lunch of hearty New England food: chowders, fish or chicken or beef, and again huge quantities of milk. After a rest period, the water sports would begin. Dinner would be at seven-thirty: again, chowders, lobster, fish, chicken, roast beef, Yorkshire pudding, mounds of ice cream, and great slabs of pie.

Rose hung an electric clock prominently in each room so that there would be no excuse for tardiness at meals. At first Eunice was in charge of all activities. Then when the children grew older, Joe hired an athletic instructor to supervise his brood. Bedtime was nine for the younger kids, ten for the others.

With his genius for picking up bargains, Joe shunned Florida real estate during the 1920s, when values were shooting sky high. Small scrub-filled lots were selling for $25,000 or more in the feverish speculation until, in 1926, the bubble burst. In 1933, when many properties were being sold for $10 or less in taxes, he bought a Spanish-style, seven-room tile-and-stucco house on "Millionaire's Row" in Palm Beach for a small sum. It stood on two acres of prime land on North Ocean Boulevard, fronted the beach, and had a swimming pool and tennis court. Rose and Joe and their family spent part of the cold months there and, after 1960, it became the President's winter White House.

Rose loved it in Palm Beach. The family gathered for Christmas, at which time a huge tree would dominate the living room, its lights reflected in the red tile of the floor. Later she became an avid golfer and devised a way of playing without paying. She would drive to the fifth tee of the Palm Beach Country Club, slip onto the course, and leave before she got to the eighteenth. "That way," Rose confided to Rita Dallas, the nurse who attended Joe following his stroke in 1961, "I don't pay a cent in green fees."

The Bronxville home was a $250,000, twenty-room Georgian-style mansion at 294 Pondfield Road, surrounded by five acres of landscaped lawns and gardens that soon became athletic fields for the hard-charging young Kennedys. More than once, Jack was knocked unconscious during touch football games and would pick himself up without help from the others, sit a while on the grass until his head cleared, then rejoin the game.

At forty-one, Joe had already accumulated $9,000,000 in liquor dealing, stock transactions, the making of cheap movies, and ownership of two large theater chains. He sold all his stock holdings before the October crash and was on his way to amassing a fortune of $400,000,000, enormous in those pre-inflation years. Years later,

Rose was reading a magazine article as she lounged beside the pool of their Palm Beach home. Looking up, she said to Joe, who was beside her, "It says here we're worth three hundred million dollars. I didn't know we had that much money."

Without putting down his newspaper, Joe replied: "You never asked."

Even though the money was rolling in during the Bronxville years, Joe wasn't letting any of it slip away easily. One day his chauffeured limousine pulled into a gasoline station a short distance from his home. Leaning out from the backseat, Joe informed the owner that another station nearby had offered him a two-cent discount on gas for all of the Kennedy automobiles. "Can you match it?" he asked.

The owner shook his head. He was sorry, but he could not offer any discounts; he had one price, and it applied to all customers. Joe ordered his chauffeur to drive on, and from that time all his cars gassed up at the rival station.

Joe did not give his children extravagant allowances. Despite his wealth, he doled out money at the going rate for the neighborhood children — a dime a week for Bobby when he was six, forty cents for twelve-year-old Jack. Jack couldn't make ends meet and, in a classic letter Joe kept, petitioned his father for a raise shortly after he joined the Boy Scouts. This little gem, oft-quoted, must be included in this volume:

It began: "A plea for a raise by Jack Kennedy. Dedicated to my father, Mr. J. P. Kennedy. Chapter 1."

The plea, with all its imperfections of grammar and spelling, went:

"My recent allowance is 40¢. This I used for aeroplanes and other playthings of childhood but now I am a scout and I put away my childish things. Before I would spend 20¢ of my 40¢ allowance and in five minutes I would have empty pockets and nothing to gain and 20¢ to lose. When I am a scout I have to buy canteens, haversacks, blankets, searchlicgs, ponchos, things that will last for years and I can always use it while I can't use chocolate marshmallow sunday ice cream and so I put in my plea for a raise of thirty cents for me to buy such things and pay my way around."

He got it. When he went off to boarding school, Joe raised him to two dollars a week.

Other kids flocked to the local movies on Saturday afternoons in the twenties and early thirties. The Kennedys didn't have to go anywhere but their own basement, where Joe had installed the first private "all-talkie" movie theater in New England, containing twenty-seven seats and a wide screen. Joe, who was producing quickie Westerns in Hollywood, got his children any film they wanted to see. Jack didn't know this at first. One day he and some friends went to town to see a Western. When Joe found out, he berated him for spending money needlessly.

Jack spoiled many of Rose's outings by getting into some kind of scrape. While they were living in the Beals Street house, she took five of her brood into the countryside to pick blueberries. As the others were racing around filling their pails, Jack got tired and sat down on a small mound. It turned out to be an anthill.

Within minutes, the ants were swarming all over him. Rose rushed him home for a thorough de-anting.

Joe insisted on punctuality at meals, but Jack was late more often than he was on time. The rule in the households was that latecomers had to start with the course being served and miss what had gone before. Many times Jack would slide into his seat when the butler was bringing out the dessert.

But he never went hungry. He'd gobble the dessert, and when the table had been cleared and the family dispersed, he would slip into the kitchen and charm the cook into giving him the rest of the meal. Joe always wondered how he could go without food but not be famished. Jack never let on he was being very well fed.

Once Jack was playing with his dogs on the pier at Hyannis when suddenly they began to race around, snapping and snarling and nipping at each other. When he could not separate them, Jack grabbed each by the neck and hurled them into the water.

Then, the shock of the water having halted the fighting, he leaped after them and hauled both dogs to the pier.

Rose, who had observed the incident, later told a friend, "This is typical of Jack. He is never afraid to plunge into the middle of a fight or a game. He is fiercely competitive and combative, but when the action is over, he is gentle and thoughtful."

Coming events cast their shadows beforehand. One Christmas, Jean, Jack's junior by nine years, snitched on him in a letter to Joe and Rose, who were wintering in Palm Beach.

"He [Jack] kissed Betty Young under the mistletoe down in the front hall," Jean wrote. She added that Jack was also disobeying Alice Cahill, the governess who was in charge of the older children. Jean's solemn recommendation to her parents: "a spanking."

It was not administered because Rose didn't believe in punishing a child unless she could observe the misdeed firsthand. Then she would swing a ruler or a coat hanger on a young Kennedy's backside. All the boys felt her wrath often. "Mother would have been a great featherweight," Ted said later. "She had a mean right hand."

Jack was an omnivorous reader. As a young man, he could flash through a massive tome in no time, and later, thanks to a speed-reading course, he was able to digest vast amounts of documents and reports handed to him overnight, amazing his staff. The interest in quality books began early. Once Kay Halle, an author and family friend, visited him at Massachusetts General Hospital in Boston.

17

"He couldn't have been more than twelve or thirteen," Halle said. "He'd had some football accident and had developed what they thought was a sort of anemia and Joe was a bit worried about it. Jack was lying in bed, very pale, which highlighted the freckles across his nose. He was so surrounded by books I could hardly see him. I was very impressed because at that point this very young child was reading *The World Crisis* by Sir Winston Churchill."

By virtue of primogeniture, Joe, Jr., demanded senior status from the other children, and got it willingly from everyone but Jack, who fought him at every turn. Firstborn or not, Joe had nothing conceded to him by Jack. Consequently, the battles were frequent, furious, and often bloody. Joe, pounds heavier and inches taller, won them all.

Once the brothers and two companions went sailing in rough seas off Hyannis Port. Joe, as skipper, ordered Jack and his friend to man the windward side of the small craft. Whenever the boat dipped low in the water, high waves driven by a stiff wind swept over Jack and his friend, who howled in anger and frustration. But the captain kept them in their painful, and very wet, posts until they landed. Onshore, Jack raced after Joe, mayhem in mind, but couldn't catch him.

Another time, Joe again the skipper by seniority, threw a mutinous Jack Kennedy overboard, then stretched out a hand and yanked him back in.

Jack's battles against Joe were like flailing against the wind. One day they raced each other on bicycles around the block, pedaling in opposite directions. The winner was to be the first to arrive back at the starting point. The race was a dead heat, but so intent was each on winning that they crashed into each other at the finish line. Jack, bleeding profusely, needed twenty-eight stitches. Joe's bike was mangled, but he himself was untouched.

Even in his early teens, Jack thought out problems carefully before acting on them. At Hyannis Port one day the family organized a treasure hunt for the children and their friends. By late evening, Jack and Joe, working as a team, lacked only one more "treasure," an old-fashioned derby hat — the kind worn by Boston pols a generation back.

The brothers took stock. One of them recalled that grandfather Honey Fitz had told them that a former Hyannis postmaster named Thomas E. Murphy had blazed a political trail by becoming the first Democrat to hold the job. Murphy, Honey Fitz said, was a strong supporter of Democrat Alfred E. Smith in the latter's Presidential race against Herbert Hoover in 1928. And Smith's trademark was a derby. Wouldn't Murphy, a Democratic Irish Catholic, have the hat they needed?

Jack and Joe sought out Murphy's son, E. Thomas Murphy, who lived in Hyannis, told him their mission, and asked if he could supply one. He could and he did, handing the brothers his father's hat. Afterward, Murphy told Leo Damore, a longtime Cape Cod resident, "What impressed my father and me more than anything else was how cleverly they had used their heads, working out the location of what must have been, at that time, just about the only derby in Hyannis."

Schooldays

Canterbury was his first boarding school and, predictably, he was homesick. He wrote home often, telling his parents what he thought of everything: the football team was "pretty bad" but the swimming pool was great; the courses were "pretty hard" and there was "a whole lot of religion"; it was "freezing at night and pretty cold in the daytime"; and the food, Rose and Joe were happy to hear, "is pretty good, better than you get in most schools."

He did not make varsity but became quarterback on the second team. The games, he said, "were not a Sunday-school picnic." About the match with the Lehen Club, he wrote [the spelling and punctuation are his]:

"You would run through their line somebody would whack you accross your face somebody else would crack your head. You would stagger, five fellows would jump on your neck. They would get you down. Then the six remaining fellows would sit on you for all sorts of reasons each one have his own particular desire.

"They had a gentle sort of fellow called Butch. He made a cushion out of a lot of fellows and I

21

seemed to be his most particular desire. The score was 20-20. I played pretty well. Making one touchdown and a point."

There were two more games left, Jack wrote. The understated humor that was to emerge strongly in later years was already evident, as he wrote: "It does not take much imagination to understand why I am looking forward to a pleasant week with the ground as hard as a rock and two heavy teams to play."

Jack was a terrible speller as a boy. His letters from school contained these gems:

"I learned to play baggamon today."

"I went out for football pracite."

"Please send me the *Litrary Digest . . .*"

"Send some choclate pie with whipt cream . . ."

He went to a church "bazar."

He made the lower-school basketball team as a "gaurd" and shot a basket, which he considered a "miricle."

After spending the winter recess with his parents in Florida, he wrote back to them: "I had the most fun of any vacation. Lining them up here they are:

"1st Florida itself

"2nd the surf

"3rd the water

"4th the fun in the pool and water

"5th learning how to play golf

"6th playing golf

"7th trip to Miami . . . Gar Woods boat

"8th Zepplin [sic] ride

"9th Hills orange grove and swimming at Gusses

"10th being able to talk about the other nine"

At Choate, the tight schedule kept him moving. He rose at ten minutes after seven to the sound of bells ringing throughout the campus and had only a quarter-hour to dress for breakfast, which was served promptly at seven twenty-five. Fifteen minutes later, he ran upstairs to fix up his room and was off to classes from eight until one.

Lunch was twenty minutes, from one-ten to one-thirty, followed by a conference with his teachers. Between three and five, he was in the gym or on the athletic fields. An hour of study was required between five-thirty and six-thirty, followed by dinner, a quarter-hour of chapel, and another two-hour study period before lights out.

Rules called for short hair; shirts, ties, and jackets were required in class and at all school events.

From the start, nobody called him John. Choate headmaster George St. John sent a bemused note to his teachers: "I don't believe Jack Kennedy knows his name is John. All the family calls him Jack, so we should do this here at school."

Jack gave his parents all sorts of explanations for his poor grades. After exhausting his list of excuses, he dreamed up the wildest one of all.

"If you study too much," he told Rose solemnly, "you're liable to go crazy." He didn't get away with it.

At Choate Jack was proudest of his accomplishments in school sports and understandably not proud at all of his academic achievements, which were unexceptional.

"In my swimming test I made 50 yards in 35 seconds," he wrote his parents. "I now am supposed to take ten laps or 250 yards a day because I am supposed to be material for a future varsity." He was elected captain of an intramural football team, the Reds, which won two games against the Grays. Noting the victory in a letter, he added: "Ahem."

When he entered upper school after his winter vacation, he aspired to be first baseman of the baseball team. "All the boys said I had first base cooked," he wrote. "When Mr. McAvoy, our French teacher, began to coach he said he remembered me from lower school. He let me pitch and by accident or else there were three terrible batters up I struck them all out. They got one run in three innings and the first two innings not a man on base. I will be modest but to tell the truth that was pretty hot so I may play pitcher or I may warm the bench."

Early on, he had an eye out for flaws in the school system that needed correcting. His first exercise in civic activity occurred when he was fifteen and a sophomore at Choate. From East Cottage, his dormitory, a narrow concrete walkway connected to the tennis courts and, beyond, the classroom buildings. More than once, Jack tripped on the path. Finally, in November, 1932, he wrote this letter to Headmaster St. John:

"The path that leads from the tennis courts down to the East Cottage has been eaten away by rain, until one-half of it is four inches higher than the other. If one walks along it at night, there is a good chance of receiving a sprained ankle. I would suggest that there be a more effecient [sic] system of drains installed near it, before the path is completely eaten away."

Shortly after St. John received the note, the path was repaired.

It's no news that teen-agers' rooms are messy, but Kennedy's was unbelievable. "Pigsty" was the term most often used to describe its condition, and no disciplinary methods against him worked for long.

During Jack's last two years at school John J. Maher, his house master, hit on a device that did have some effect. When Mr. Maher, a tough football coach and history teacher, was dissatisfied, which was nearly always, he would sweep everything Jack owned into one huge mound in the center of the room. On his return, Jack would have to sort out all his books, sports equipment, sheets, pillows, blankets, and everything else, and place them in some semblance of order. Soon he got tired of the job and kept his room in reasonably good shape.

Rules were much stricter in those years. Going downtown after class was restricted to once weekly for juniors, twice for seniors. The younger boys were not permitted into town at all without a very valid excuse. Jack Kennedy found his way to the shops with greater frequency than the regulations allowed.

Often he'd wander into Oliver D. Foote's soda shop on Center Street, the main shopping area. Mr. Foote, a tiny moustached man who made his own ice cream, had a specialty, a concoction called chocolate mousse: vanilla ice cream, chocolate syrup, and whipped cream topped with chocolate shot, now called sprinkles. It cost twenty cents and Jack gobbled the creation as often as he could.

He astonished his classmates with his memory for facts and figures. A popular radio show in those days was a quiz program called "Information Please," in which a regular panel of experts was asked questions sent in by listeners. Jack was able to answer even the toughest ones as soon as the host, Clifton Fadiman, asked them and before the experts had a chance to reply.

"Hey, Jack," one boy asked, "how do you know so much about these things?"

He replied, "I guess I read a lot."

He could talk his way out of trouble most of the time, with a smile and an outrageous story. One Sunday night he showed up for dinner looking terrible. His pants were torn, his jacket muddy, and his hair plastered with perspiration over his dirt-streaked forehead.

Sunday evening meals were always formal occasions at Choate, so William Shute, head of the math department and a strict disciplinarian, stopped him and demanded an explanation.

"Well, you see, sir," Jack replied earnestly, "Ed's horse threw him and ran away, and we had a heck of a time catching him. He ran us all over the grounds." Noting that Jack was breathing hard, Mr. Shute waved him inside.

Later, the teacher realized he had been duped. To a colleague, he said, "He didn't lie at all. He chased the horse all right, but I didn't have the brains to ask *what time*! He caught the horse in mid-afternoon, then played touch football for hours until just before dinner."

Mr. Shute, who died some years ago, recorded the story on tape now filed in the school's archives.

Kennedy had one illness after another, beginning in childhood and continuing through prep school and college. Says Harold L. Tinker, his English teacher at Choate, "He was in the infirmary more than in class." He suffered feverish colds, sinus attacks, conjunctivitis, mumps, boils, painful knees, and fallen arches.

To build up his strength, Rose asked Choate to give him a teaspoon of Kepler's Malt and cod-liver oil after every meal and to enroll him in a special class designed for "bodybuilding." His arch problems were doubtless caused or worsened, Rose wrote, because "he has persisted in wearing cheap rubber-soled shoes for the last two or three years." She asked the school to make him get good footwear with built-in supports.

Rose insisted that Jack have an egg every day, mixed into milk, a concoction he hated. But parental orders were orders, so he showed up in the dining room daily for the eggnog. The future President pinched his nose between thumb and forefinger, screwed up his face, and gulped down the stuff.

The first symptoms of a mysterious, and seemingly serious, illness appeared in his sophomore year. He felt weak and was unable to run any distance, let alone play football. He ate little, losing his appetite even for Oliver Foote's famous chocolate mousse. Often he would nod off in class.

He was poked, prodded, and tested, but nothing showed up, and in a few months the symptoms went away, only to return the next year, at which time the tests were again negative. More sophisticated examinations performed at a New Haven hospital again could not find any cause. Puzzled and somewhat worried, Rose insisted Jack come to Palm Beach in January, but weeks in the sun did little to rebuild his strength. Now alarmed, Rose and Joe sent Jack to the Mayo Clinic in Rochester, Minnesota, for thorough testing.

A week of rigorous examinations that summer still disclosed no reason for the fatigue, weight loss, and lack of appetite. He returned to Choate in the fall, rail-thin, barred from rigorous athletics for the entire year.

Eventually the weakness vanished as mysteriously as it had manifested itself. The explanation did not come to light until years later, when it was discovered that John Kennedy had a potentially life-threatening disease that the family hid from the world throughout his political career.

On February 22, 1932, Rose gave birth to her ninth and last child at St. Margaret's Hospital in Dorchester. At Choate, Jack was told of the happy event and dashed off a quick note to his mother. He was in such a hurry he forgot to sign it.

> It is the night before exams so I will
> write you Wednesday. Lots of love.
> P.S. Can I be godfather to the baby?

The following month, he came down from school and made the Profession of Faith as his newest brother was baptized Edward Moore Kennedy.

Recuperating from one of his many colds, Jack was released from the school infirmary but was ordered to remain in his dorm for several days. Bored, unhappy, looking for excitement, he wandered through the empty house — and an idea struck.

He collected dozens of pillows and mattresses from the rooms and stacked them ceiling-high in the room of a boy he didn't like. It took a couple of hours of pulling and tugging, but when he was finished nothing could fit inside the room, much less the unfortunate young man who inhabited it. When he returned, he found himself facing a wall of bedding.

Like father, like daughter. Lem Billings told that story to Caroline years afterward. When she herself went to boarding school at Concord Academy in Massachusetts, she enlisted a friend to pull the same stunt on a classmate. It worked fine.

When he was seventeen, John Kennedy stood at a crossroads. He was involved in a prank that snowballed far beyond anything he intended, and may well have been, according to Rose Kennedy, "a turning point in his life." The episode was ridiculous, but was prompted by a deep-seated rebelliousness that could have sent him in a far different direction than the one that eventually led to the Presidency.

As a teen-ager, he had a problem many families have encountered. Believing himself unable to match the accomplishments of Joe, Jr., he did what many younger siblings do — he stopped trying. He sought attention in an unacceptable way by actively fomenting rebellion against the Choate administration.

In Westerly, Rhode Island, Dr. Seymour St. John, who succeeded his father as headmaster in 1947, recalled: "Joe was the golden boy. He did everything right. Jack was younger, smaller, less organized, able in a different way. So there was an immediate invidious comparison in Jack's mind, which I think grated on him.

"He wanted terribly to make his mark. He had an overwhelming ambition and drive, but his size and strength were insurmountable handicaps. He was too small for any varsity team. Nor could he make it in student government in a popular election for office. Boys choose strong, confident persons, the very opposite of what Jack was.

"Because he couldn't make it as an athlete or in student government, he did what many young people facing a similar problem do — he went into rebellion, just total rebellion."

His schoolwork, never distinguished, worsened. In French, said his teacher, Hugh Packard, "he was frequently unprepared and his homework was sloppy and badly done." He squeezed through with a 65 in his sophomore year. In Latin, he did hardly better, with a 69.

"Passing but poor," said his teacher, Owen Morgan. "He'd try to bluff hell out of me," Mr. Morgan said. "When I called on him, he'd rise, strike a stance, and boldly launch into a translation as though he'd worked on a passage for hours, but he'd soon bomb out."

In French class, he conspired with two friends to con the teacher with a split-the-assignment trick. Each boy would prepare only one-third of the lesson, then volunteer to recite the section he knew. It worked for a while and Jack Kennedy was racking up great grades until the teacher caught on.

The climax came in Jack's senior year.

Headmaster St. John, a stickler for discipline, would often refer to badly misbehaving students as "muckers," which the dictionary describes as a "rough, coarse person." Anyone who fell below the behavioral standards expected of a Choate boy was a mucker. Students who sneaked off to New Haven to visit girl friends — or, worse those who smoked in dorms, cheated on exams, destroyed property — all were muckers.

"To be called a mucker was just about the lowest thing there was," says Seymour St. John.

Listening to an anti-mucker lecture in chapel one afternoon, Jack Kennedy conceived an idea. He called together a dozen cronies in his room and, with Lem Billings, organized a club. And what more delightfully perverse thought than to call it the Muckers Club"?

31

Gleefully, the boys visited a local jeweler and had little gold charms made for themselves, each inscribed: "Choate Muckers Club."

Says Seymour St. John, "It was more funny than activist, nothing like the militancy of later years. But it *was* a ridiculing of the establishment and, when he heard about it, my father was furious."

Headmaster St. John wrote to Joe Kennedy in Washington: I think you and Jack and I ought to have a three-cornered talk. Could you come up here?" Busy as he was, Joe Kennedy went.

The scene that afternoon in the headmaster's study was memorable. Joe, whose temper was legendary, ripped into his son. And when he let up, St. John began.

Recalled Seymour St. John, "My father laid it on the line to Jack Kennedy: If he didn't respond, if he didn't shape up, he faced expulsion from school. The choice was made crystal clear to him — if he was to stay on at Choate, he would have to change his ways.

"It was a watershed for the boy. From this point on, Jack Kennedy would either go in the right direction or the wrong one."

Shaken, Jack promised to dissolve the Muckers and tow the line.

Few boys want to be saddled with an uncomplimentary nickname; fewer still voluntarily adopt one. It was a measure of young Jack's rebelliousness that he flaunted the name hung earlier on Joe and heartily despised by him. Because of his thin, narrow features, Joe had been dubbed Rat Face by the students. Hating it, he would swing on any kid who addressed him that way.

Jack inherited the name and perversely gloried in it. Said Hugh Packard, "He took pride in it."

And Lem Billings added, "He put it under his picture in the yearbook, *The Brief*, in 1935."

Major events at Choate were the spring and winter festivals, when boys were permitted to invite girls for a weekend of tea, dancing, and proms. His friends and former teachers do not recall seeing Jack Kennedy at any of them until the last year. Said Hugh Packard, "He was not a lounge lizard." The expression, popular in the twenties and thirties, meant "ladies' man."

Kennedy lost his virginity at the age of eighteen, just prior to his graduation from Choate, in a Harlem whorehouse, where he went with two classmates, Ralph "Rip" Horton and Lem Billings.

John Kennedy rigged his first election campaign.

In senior year, he was voted "most likely to succeed" by his class, a fact that Rose proudly recorded in her autobiography, *Times to Remember*. While Jack's winning smile and personal charm attracted friends, he had been in trouble regularly, had never run for class office, and few of his teachers could spot any latent intellectualism in the modest grades he drew. Why, then, did the graduating class honor him with that distinction?

The truth is that the fix was in. Kennedy conspired with Horton to lobby for him, and Rip did a good job. In return for his help, J.F.K. scrawled a message on the class senior portrait, which he presented to Horton: "To Boss Tweed from Honest Abe, pray we room together at Sing Sing."

If Jack's family was delighted, the Choate faculty was astounded. "If you had asked the teachers where Kennedy would stand," declared Seymour St. John, "I'd expect they would have put him well below the middle."

St. John's explanation of the vote was that it had to be "a gag" on the students' part. They probably thought, he said, "Here's a guy who has been anti-establishment. Let's put him up for it."

Here is John Kennedy's complete course of study at Choate, with the names of his teachers, the dormitories in which he lived, and the extracurricular activities in which he participated. *The Brief* was the name of the school yearbook.

1931–1932 Third Former

English 3	Frank D. Gurll
French IC	Ben Davis
Latin 3	Paul A. Warren
Algebra 1	Hallett N. Lewis

Sports: 1st term: League Football
2nd term: League Basketball
3rd term: League Baseball
House: Choate House — Mr. Earl G. Leinbach

1932–1933 Fourth Former

English 4	John J. Maher
Latin (Caesar)	Owen H. Morgan
French 2	Hugh S. Packard
Algebra 2F	Earl G. Leinbach
	Activities: *Brief* Board

Sports: 1st term: League Football
2nd term: II Basketball Squad
3rd term: Crew
House: East Cottage — Mr. Eugene F. Musser

1933–1934 Fifth Former

English 5B	Harold L. Tinker
French 3G	Ben Davis
Plane Geometry 4	Charles W. Collins
History A	Russell R. Ayres
	Activities: *Brief* Board

Sports: 1st term: Junior Football
2nd term: II Basketball Squad
3rd term: Apparatus
House: West Wing — Mr. John J. Maher

1934–1935 Sixth Former

English 6	Dudley Fitts
French 4B	Edwin Proctor
Physics	H. Dayton Niehaus
History CH	George C. St. John, Jr.
Public Speaking	Stanley Pratt
	Activities: *Brief* Business Manager

Sports: not allowed, due to illness
House: West Wing — Mr. John J. Maher

Jack graduated with a C average, and most of his teachers expressed the opinion that the grade was far below his true intelligence and potential.

The summer after he graduated from Choate, Jack Kennedy spent a night in jail with his brother Joe.

Each year the Edgartown Yacht Club sponsors a regatta over an eighteen-mile course around the triangular island of Martha's Vineyard, off Cape

Cod. The race attracts many thousands of visitors and was in those years just as noteworthy for its post-sailing fun and games as for the event itself. The upper-class young people who lived on the mainland used the regatta as a prime excuse for getting roaring drunk at parties on yachts and in hotels and lodging houses.

Sailing was one of John Kennedy's passions. By 1934, though only seventeen, he had already won several trophies. The following summer, at six feet tall, wiry, and in decent health for a change, he and Joe went to Edgartown for the regatta.

They brought vast quantities of food and liquor to an Edgartown hotel and, after the race, hosted a party for a large group of friends. The subsequent boisterousness alarmed the manager. He investigated and was even more upset by the damage that was being inflicted on the property.

The manager called the police, who hauled Joe and Jack off to the town's tiny jail. In the morning, the boys were allowed to go home when the hotel management said it would not press charges.

By 1969, the rowdiness of former years had quieted down, but parties were still being held on the Vineyard and on another, smaller island to the east, Chappaquiddick. It was there, of course, that Ted Kennedy, driving away from a cookout, in a black Oldsmobile, plunged off a crude wooden bridge. Mary Joe Kopechne, one of six young women at the party, who was riding with Kennedy, was drowned.

Chapter Two

Harvard and London

Vacationing at Hyannis Port the summer after gradua-
tion, Jack pondered where to continue his education. He
vacillated between Princeton, where his good friends
Lem and Rip were enrolled, and Harvard, his father's
alma mater and where brother Joe again was a big man
on campus. Jack applied to both.

College was postponed for a year, however, when Joe
Kennedy decided that Jack, again like Joe, should study
with Professor Harold Laski, world-renowned socialist
who taught at the London School of Economics. Jack
went to London in September, 1935, with his parents
and sister, Kathleen, and was enrolled in Laski's classes.
Barely one month later, he was ill again and had to with-
draw. In November he returned home to enter Princeton
about six weeks after the term had begun. He roomed
with Billings and Horton in South Reunion Hall in in-
expensive lodgings (all that Billings could afford) where
the bathroom was in the basement.

Stricken again in December with what was diagnosed as jaundice, Jack spent two months at Peter Bent Brigham Hospital in Boston. He dropped out of Princeton and went to Arizona to convalesce at the Jay Six ranch, run by a friend of Arthur Krock, political correspondent and columnist for The New York Times.

In the fall of 1936 he followed Joe, Jr., to Harvard, where the old rivalry continued. Again, Joe outshone Jack in almost everything from grades to sports to personal popularity. Two years later, when his father was named American ambassador to the Court of St. James's, Jack obtained a six-month leave from school and sailed to London to work as his secretary. He spent much of his time traveling to France, Russia, Palestine, Greece, and Germany, where he talked to government leaders and reported back to his father on their attitudes. This early experience gave John Kennedy an invaluable world view.

Back at Harvard, he worked on his honors thesis, which later became a best-selling book. After getting his degree in June, 1940, he enrolled in the Stanford University Business School for graduate study but dropped out after a few months. When spring came, he attempted to enlist in the army because brother Joe was a naval aviation cadet and Jack was weary of competition. The doctors rejected him because of a spinal injury he had suffered during a football scrimmage at Harvard.

After a five-month exercise-and-therapy program, Jack applied to the navy and was accepted. Once more he was chasing his brother Joe, who was on his way to winning his wings.

Girls and a Best Seller

At Harvard one of his main interests was the pursuit of girls, most of whom he caught.

By the time he reached his junior year, his sexual urges were being amply satisfied, as he wrote his friend Lem Billings in Princeton. "I can now get tail as often and as free as I want which is a step in the right direction," he said, referring to previous liaisons in bordellos.

In January, 1938, he planned a visit to Lem and asked for a room as far as possible from the other students and especially from Billings's girl friend. "I don't want you coming in for a chat in the middle as usual and discussing how sore your cock is," Jack wrote.

Jack's academic average was midway between a B, and a C, improving as he went along. As a freshman he earned a B in economics but pulled C's in history, French, and English. The next year was worse: four C's, a B, and a dismal D. Junior year was better, with a C and five B's, and as a senior he received B's in all courses.

After Jack attended Joe's commencement in Cambridge, the two brothers sailed back to England aboard the French liner *Normandie*. Each had no trouble finding girl friends, and each was returning to the Kennedy suite in the very early hours. Father Joe didn't like that at all. "From now on," he told them, you boys will be back at midnight, no later." The brothers obediently said they would comply, but they knew something their father did not. There were two entrances to the suite — one was from the main deck, and the second was a service door located far from the bedrooms, which led into a narrow passageway.

So every night, Jack and Joe came back before the deadline, satisfying their father, but in a short while they would tiptoe to the service door and resume their partying in the ship's salons, returning the same way, long after their father was asleep.

Besides girls, Jack's preoccupation was the same as it had been at Choate, athletics, but here, too, his reach exceeded his grasp.

In football he made the junior varsity team in his sophomore year, but he was forced to drop out because of a spinal injury. He won a place on the swimming team but didn't get his letter because he failed to compete against Yale in the biggest meet of the year. (At Harvard, letters are awarded to team members who played in the traditional encounters against Yale.) A short time before the trials that would determine the makeup of the Harvard team, Jack had come down with the flu. With his roommate's connivance, he slipped out at night several times to practice in the pool, with predictable results. He became weaker and did poorly in the trials.

Nor was he successful in school politics. He ran for president of his freshman class with thirty-five other candidates and trailed far behind the leaders. As a sophomore he sought a place on the student council, but couldn't round up enough votes to be put on the ballot. Finally, in his last year, he won his only elective post as a member of the six-man Permanent Class Committee.

Afterward a story circulated that J.F.K.'s classmates, by some means of clairvoyance, saw in him the brilliance that foreshadowed his future as a world leader. In fact, they saw nothing of the kind. Declared classmate Cleveland Amory, the author, "The legend is pure hogwash."

"You can take the boy out of Irish Boston," wrote Joe McCarthy, a journalist who was a lifelong friend of the Kennedy family, "but apparently it is difficult to take the Irish Boston out of the boy."

At Harvard, Jack's roommate was Torbert Macdonald, an Irish Catholic from a middle-class family; Bobby's best friend was Kenneth P. O'Donnell, whose father had coached the Holy Cross football team, and Joe, Jr.'s, closest pal was Ted Reardon, who had to work his way through school.

These friendships were significant. Jack, like his brothers, never tried to climb socially, although he had every chance, having associated all through prep school with sons of wealthy families, many of them listed in the Social Register.

Old Joe had wanted to escape his roots; Jack, perhaps subconsciously, returned to them. All his life he was most comfortable with people like Torby, Ted, and Kenny.

That explains why, when he became President, he worked best with, and trusted most, his "Irish Mafia."

In those days, Jack was selective when it came to girls. Afterward, he would become less choosy.

As a student, "Jack worked on quality," said Lem Billings. His own goal, Lem admitted, was quantity.

During his campaign for the Presidency, one journalist observed, Jack "bedded any female who wasn't a complete turnoff, and his standards were low." Reporters covering him often saw him sneaking down the stairs in his hotel for a liaison.

Because of this, they pinned a label on him that persisted in the inner circles for years. It was "Jack the Zipper."

After freshman year, Jack toured Europe with Lem, but not in style. Since Billings, whose father had died while he was at Choate, had little money, Jack scaled down his own living costs. He could afford the continent's finest hostelries, but for three months stayed at bed-and-breakfast homes and the cheapest tourist hotels they could find, often spending less than fifty cents a day.

Never in the history of Harvard did so many important persons contribute so much to help an undergraduate achieve such a great success with his honors thesis.

It began with the less than snappy title: *Appeasement at Munich: The Inevitable Result of the Slowness of Conversion of the British Democracy from a Disarmament to a Rearmament Policy*, and ended as a book that sold an amazing 80,000 copies and earned Jack $40,000 in royalties.

The thesis charged that England had not prepared for World War II with Germany, and included interviews with world leaders, arranged for Jack by his father. Few other seniors had such access to persons who could contribute valuable information, as well as to vital official British records.

Jack's paper ran to 150 pages, for which he needed the help of a professional typist. As his deadline approached, he asked Torby to place a want ad in a Boston newspaper. Problems quickly arose. First, in those days, Harvard had strict rules that barred women from the men's rooms. And second, as a gag, Torby had stated in the ad that the typist had to be "young."

With the scarcity of part-time jobs around the campus, it was little wonder that dozens of women — young, as specified — converged on Winthrop House, the old red-brick structure facing the Charles River where the school's athletes roomed. Jack had to explain their presence to authorities and solemnly promised none would invade his living area upstairs.

Usually, honors theses are deposited in Widener Library at Harvard, reposing there forgotten and unseen over the years. Joe Kennedy, however, had other plans for Jack's study. He persuaded Arthur Krock to take steps to have it published. Jack journeyed to Washington, where he and the *Times* pundit edited the manuscript, removing its academic tone and, at Krock's suggestion, changing the title to the more commercial *Why England Slept*, a satirical dig at Winston Churchill, who had published a book called *While England Slept*.

Next it was put in the hands of a top literary agent, while Joe set about convincing Henry R. Luce, a Republican and head of the powerful Time-Life company, to write a foreword. After it was sold to the publishing firm of Wilfrid Funk, Inc., Joe alerted his friends that the book was on its way.

It was published in July, 1940, and earned rave reviews. Said the *New Yorker*: "The young son of Ambassador Kennedy contributes a cool and factual study of the complex reasons underlying England's failure to rearm during the thirties and traces a warning parallel between our own situation now and England's up to now."

The New York Times called it "a book of such painstaking scholarship, such mature understanding and fair-mindedness and of such penetrating and timely conclusions that it is a notable textbook for our times."

Wrote *The Times* of London: "It is a young man's book; it contains much wisdom for older men."

By September, Jack Kennedy, at twenty-three, was a best-selling author, caught up in the frenzy of marketing his own book. He autographed copies, submitted to radio and press interviews, answered letters from admirers, and — as all writers do — called up bookstores to see if they had it and, if they did not, urged the publisher to send copies. "They're going like hot cakes," he told Charles Spalding. He contributed his British earnings to charity and bought himself a new car with the money he made in the U.S.

Jack had bested his brother Joe at last. His agent, Gertrude Algase, wrote to him that even though Joe had achieved a measure of political fame at the 1940 convention, when he had been a delegate, Jack had "stolen the thunder" with his book, though quite innocently. Algase also wanted to know if Jack had any ideas for another book.

Jack loved it.

One summer late in the 1950s, Henry Luce was a guest on William Benton's yacht. Benton, a former Democratic senator from Connecticut, was chairman of the board of the *Encyclopedia Britannica*. He noticed that Luce was spending part of each day writing busily on deck. Curious, he approached him one afternoon and asked, "What are you writing?"

Replied Luce, "I'm rewriting the preface I did for Jack's book, *Why England Slept*.

Benton, aware that the association of Republican Luce and Democrat Kennedy was indeed an odd one, asked, "How did you happen to do it to begin with?

"He gave me a three-letter word for an answer," Benton recalled, "and you won't have to guess much what the word was.

"The word was 'Joe.'"

Ambassador's Son

Joe Kennedy, Sr., had a salty vocabulary that he didn't clean up even when talking to a President of the United States.

After Roosevelt's election in 1932, he named Joe the first chairman of the newly created Securities and Exchange Commission, then appointed him head of the Maritime Commission, in which capacity Joe ordered sailors who had mutinied on a merchant vessel to be placed in irons.

Roosevelt was shocked. He phoned Kennedy in New York and told him that his order smacked of medievalism and should be rescinded. Joe objected strongly. Crews on ships at sea must behave by the rules, he said, or face severe discipline. F.D.R. kept arguing for leniency, Joe for discipline.

Finally Joe lost his temper. A loose policy, he said, would be counter-productive. He told the President bluntly, "Listen, boy, if we do that [give up strict enforcement] we'll land in the shit house."

When Robert Worth Bingham, U.S. ambassador to Great Britain, died in 1937, Roosevelt offered the post to Joe Kennedy. The career men in the State Department were astounded. "A bad, bad, choice," said one high-ranking diplomat. It was felt that Joe, an irascible, trigger-tempered, blunt-speaking Irish Catholic, would be like the proverbial bull in the china shop at the Court of St. James's. But Roosevelt was undeterred. He named Joe.

Shortly afterward, Roosevelt introduced Kennedy to then Secretary of State Cordell Hull at the White House. Joe, as usual, had a story. A few days earlier, he said, his friend Arthur Krock had expressed shock that Hugo Black, just named to the Supreme Court, had not told Roosevelt that in his youth he had been a member of the Ku Klux Klan in Alabama.

F.D.R. asked Joe, "When Krock said that, what did you say to him."

Replied Joe, "If Marlene Dietrich asked you to make love to her, would you tell her you weren't much good at making love?"

Roosevelt guffawed and staid, white-haired Hull looked as though he swallowed a fish bone. Later, Joe said, "Hull must have been saying to himself, 'My God, is this the kind of guy we're going to send to the Court of St. James's?'"

The new ambassador and his large family fascinated the Brits. The *Daily Express*, owned by Joe's friend, Lord Beaverbrook, heralded his arrival in 1938 with the headline: "Nine Children and Nine Million Dollars."

Another paper called him "The U.S.A. Nine-Child Envoy."

Joe arrived in February with his two oldest daughters, Rosemary and Kathleen, who were twenty and eighteen, respectively, but Rose, hospitalized with an appendectomy, could not join him until the following month. Jack and Joe, Jr., still at Harvard, were the only Kennedys left in the States when Rose sailed to England with Teddy, then six, Bobby, twelve, Eunice, seventeen, Patricia, fourteen, and Jean, ten.

The new ambassador, trailed by reporters, came down to Plymouth Harbour to meet his family, arriving on the S.S. *Washington*. As they walked to the train station after disembarking, Joe reached into his pocket and took out one ticket — for his own return trip to London. He had forgotten to buy tickets for his wife and children. He patted his pockets; no wallet, either.

The $9,000,000 ambassador had to borrow $120 from newsmen to get his family to their new home.

The Kennedys occupied a thirty-six-room, six-story mansion at 14 Princes Gate, opposite Kensington Gardens. It had eight baths and eight bedrooms for the family, and thirteen bedrooms and baths on the top two floors for the servants.

The house became Hyannis Port East the first day, when Teddy became fascinated with the electric elevator and rode it up and down all afternoon. Day after day he jockeyed the lift, often neglecting to close both the inner and outer doors when he left. This made it impossible to summon the elevator until someone mounted the stairs and shut the doors. Joe finally grounded him.

Telephones that connected every room were constantly in use as the kids jabbered about anything and everything. They raced through the vast rooms, chasing one another, looking for things or just because it was fun to race. It got worse toward late afternoon when, arriving home from school, they brought friends to play. Once a visitor saw a goldfish in the tub. It belonged to Teddy, who had found it gasping in its bowl. In an attempt to revive it, he had tossed it into a larger body of water.

Sometimes the kids had trouble in their new schools. On her first day, Jean made a mistake in an arithmetic problem. When her teacher pointed out the error, Jean bristled. "Five goes into nine twice in America," she said. I don't see why it doesn't in England!"

Not long after his arrival as the new ambassador, Joe Kennedy hit a hole in one at the Stoke Poges Golf Club. Accorded the customary acclaim for the meritorious feat, he made a comment that won headlines and editorial approval in the British press: "I'm much happier," he said, "being the father of nine children and making a hole in one than I would be as the father of one child making a hole in nine."

In the summer of 1938, Kathleen, by then a belle in London society, secured for Jack and Joe an invitation to one of the season's swankiest coming-out parties. Held in an elegant Mayfair town house, the guests included the cream of Britain's young people, most of them titled nobility, all of them rich.

Jack made his way to the ballroom and quickly spotted an exceptionally beautiful young woman on the dance floor. Unaware of the protocol at British debutante parties, he was about to cut in when a strong hand gripped his shoulder. "Just a moment, sonny," said one of the guests, "you'll dance when it's your turn."

Chagrined, Jack learned the rules. Young men were given numbers with the names of female guests and waited until the numbers came around before they could dance with the young ladies. The pretty one got away. "To make matters worse," Jack said later, "they picked two of the plainest girls there for our partners."

Next day, he and Joe left for the Continent and spent the summer in the south of France, and Italy.

Joe, Sr., was plagued by stomach problems most of his life. Periodically he sent samples of his stool to Dr. Sara Jordan, the noted gastroenterologist of the Lahey Clinic in Boston, for examination. To make sure she received them fast, he had them delivered by diplomatic pouch, prompting some embassy staff members to comment: "There go some more of Ambassador Kennedy's reports to the States."

Despite his father's right-wing conservatism, seeds of the liberal principles of John Kennedy's administration were starting to show green shoots by the time he was twenty-one. Luella Hennessey Donovan, the Kennedy family nurse, remembered this story:

In the summer of 1938, Joe took his family for a vacation in Cannes, on the French Riviera. He rented a large villa overlooking the Mediterranean, where five of the young Kennedys — Eunice, Pat, Jean, Bobby, and Ted — had a great time swimming and hurtling around as they did at Hyannis Port.

Jack had been studying and traveling in Europe for part of his junior year and had come down from London to spend a few days with the family. One stormy afternoon, a fire was lit in the large sitting room of the villa, and the five young Kennedys sat around as their older brother talked to them about the lessons of history.

He held them spellbound as he told them stories about Hannibal, the brilliant young statesman and general of ancient Carthage; of Julius Caesar, the conqueror and dictator of the Roman Empire, and Napoleon.

"All three," Jack said, "were dictatorial rulers whose nations won great renown but at terrible cost, because the people over whom they ruled did not share in the glory. They received nothing. And so eventually the people revolted against these three dictators and threw them out of power. But then, other strong men arose to grasp the reins. And this continued until these once-glorious nations were glorious no longer. They shriveled and died.

"But now look at the United States. It is the most powerful country in the world. Why?" He paused, and his small audience, enraptured by his accounts, shook their heads. "Because," Jack continued, "power lay in the people. The people themselves make their laws through their elected representatives, enforce them, govern themselves. And so the great question for all Americans is how to avoid the great mistakes that had led to the downfall of other nations."

Declares Luella, who was herself riveted by Jack's eloquence, "As I listened to him, I thought with amazement: Why, he's only twenty one. Imagine this young man talking so passionately about these great principles. Other young men his age would be having a good time with the girls, but he's here, with his brothers and sisters, talking so simply and clearly about the lessons of history that even a little boy like Teddy, who was only six, could understand and want to hear more."

Jack had already begun to question his father's social conservatism. At the dinner table, there was little discussion of money and business; it was politics and policies that excited the entire family, even the younger children. Joe, to his credit, always encouraged his brood to face up to him and argue their points.

Joe, Jr., did precisely that in the late 1930s. He claimed that F.D.R.'s New Deal, which aimed at using the authority of the government to help economically deprived groups, was essential to lift the nation out of the Great Depression. Joe, Sr., felt the country was on its way to socialism, endangering its capitalistic structure. His son Jack thought that was nonsense and answered back forcefully.

Seated next to Joe, Jr., Jack listened carefully. One day, after a particularly sharp argument, he told Rose, "You know, Mother, Joe seems to understand the situation better than Dad."

Hitler invaded Poland on September 1, 1939, and two days later England and France declared war on Germany. Joe Kennedy took immediate steps to move his family to the English countryside to avoid the bombs he knew would soon rain on London.

Britain's affection for the rambunctious Joe cooled measurably as his isolationist and defeatist views became increasingly pronounced. Less than seven weeks after the outbreak of hostilities, Joe made a speech commemorating Admiral Horatio Nelson's defeat of the combined French and Spanish fleets off Cape Trafalgar in 1805, in which he said: "It is true that the democratic and dictator countries have important and fundamental divergencies of outlook, which in certain areas go deeper than politics. But there is simply no sense, common or otherwise, in letting these differences grow into unremitting antagonisms. After all, we have to live together in the same world, whether we like it or not."

Britain, having cast off appeasement policies, was in no mood to hear isolationist remarks. A barrage of criticism followed. The assaults grew in intensity as the war went on, and by the following year the British had become thoroughly disenchanted with the tart-tongued Joe.

Winston Churchill, hearing from Kennedy's own lips his view that the British could not win, wanted him removed from his post. By this time, the Prime Minister had become so infuriated with

Joe's attitude that he was bypassing him in official communications and dealing directly with President Roosevelt.

In October, 1940, Joe flew home on the Dixie Clipper. The day he left, he was presented with an air-raid siren to remind him of embattled London. Said Kennedy, "It's going to come in handy back home. I'm going to use it at Hyannis Port to call the children in from their boats at dinner time."

Within weeks of his arrival back in the States, Joe blew the ambassadorship because he couldn't keep his mouth shut.

A few days after F.D.R. was reelected, Joe was staying at the Ritz-Carlton Hotel in Boston. Louis Lyons of the *Boston Globe* asked for an interview. "Sure," Joe said. "Come on up." Already in the suite were two other newsmen, Ralph Coglan and Charles Edmondson, of the *St. Louis Post Dispatch*.

In shirt-sleeves, his suspenders flapping around his waist, Joe began talking between bites of apple pie topped with cheese. With no diplomatic restraint whatsoever, he delivered his opinions of the war and the country to which he was U.S. envoy. And they were blistering.

He was willing to spend every cent he had to keep America out of the war, he said, "because there's no sense in our getting in." Democracy, he declared, was "finished" in Great Britain, adding: "It isn't that she's fighting for democracy. That's the bunk. She's fighting for self-preservation, just as we will if it comes to us. As long as she can hold out, give her what it takes, whatever we don't have to have, and don't expect anything back."

The only favorable comment he had about England was made about Queen Elizabeth, the present queen's mother. "She is one of the most intelligent women you ever met," he said. "She's got more brains than the cabinet."

He also made a savage assault on Eleanor Roosevelt. "She bothered us more on our jobs in Washington to take care of the poor little nobodies than all of the rest of the people down there put together, " he said. "She's always sending me a note to have some little Susie Glotz to tea at the embassy."

He also castigated American congressmen as "dopes who don't understand the war or our relationship to it."

Two days later, everything hit the fan. Joe thought he was speaking off the record, but Lyons, who said he had not made this clear, published the entire damning interview, complete with all the colorful phrases. It also appeared in newspapers around the country and the world.

The British were enraged, many Americans hardly less so. Roosevelt said, "I never want to see that son-of-a-bitch again."

Joe's efforts to disavow the interview failed, and he was forced to resign.

His own career in government and politics finished, Joe returned to what he knew best, making money and creating the Kennedy phenomenon in America.

Chapter Three

First Affair and a Hero's Medal

Jack Kennedy was commissioned as an ensign in the U.S. Naval Reserve on September 25, 1941. His father called a few friends and Jack was assigned to the Office of Naval Intelligence in Washington, where he mostly wrote and edited bulletins for both high navy personnel and ship and shore stations.

A romance with Danish-born Inga Arvad resulted in a transfer to the Sixth Naval District Headquarters in Charleston, South Carolina. In July, 1942, he was assigned to sea duty and sent to the U.S. Naval Reserve Midshipman's School at Northwestern University, Evanston, Illinois, where he was taught seamanship. After completing the three-month training, he was promoted to lieutenant, junior grade, and sent to Melville, Rhode Island, where the navy was training officers for PT boats.

In March, 1943, Kennedy was sent to the Solomon Islands in the Pacific Ocean, where, one month later, he took over command of PT 109. On the morning of August 2, PT 109 was rammed by a Japanese destroyer. Kennedy's bravery in that action earned for him the Navy and Marine Medal, his feat later memorialized in several books, magazine stories, and a motion picture.

Back in action after a short time, Jack took over command of PT 59 and was later transferred to a Miami shore installation. With the recurrence of back problems, he was sent to Chelsea Naval Hospital in Boston. He was convalescing from back surgery at the family compound in Hyannis Port when word came of the death of Joe, Jr., which changed his place in the family and his life.

Still in great pain, Kennedy officially retired from the navy because of his disabled back. Joe Kennedy, Sr., up to his old tricks, again called a friend, this time publisher William Randolph Hearst, and Jack got a dream newspaper assignment.

Love and War

As 1941 was drawing to a close, Jack became involved in a love affair that almost got him cashiered out of the navy. A discharge in all likelihood would have ended his political career before it had begun.

He was twenty-four and Inga Arvad was twenty-eight when they were introduced in Washington by Arthur Krock. A startlingly beautiful blue-eyed honey blonde, Inga was a free spirit with an outgoing, effervescent personality that matched his own sense of fun and captivated him from the start. She was no one-night stand, as most of his other playmates were (out of his mind as soon as they were out of his bed), but a woman who, despite her bubbly nature, was intelligent, perceptive, and never boring.

A traveler in the international set, Inga at various times had dated William Cavendish, the Marquess of Hartington, who later married his sister Kick, and Hugh Fraser, who would soon become a member of Parliament. But she was suspected of having other connections, too, and that was where the trouble lay.

As a Danish journalist in the early 1930s, she had interviewed German Reich marshal Hermann Göring several times and had been invited to his wedding, where the best man was the Führer, Adolf Hitler. She had also interviewed Joseph Goebbels, the Nazi propaganda minister, and Hitler himself. She had been a guest at a dinner party given by Göring, and in 1936 was invited to accompany Hitler to the summer Olympics in Berlin.

Small wonder that when she came to America to work for the *Washington Times-Herald*, the Federal Bureau of Investigation placed her under surveillance, a fact unknown, of course, to Ensign John Kennedy, U.S.N. He did know , however, that Inga was married at the time to Paul Fejos, a Hungarian film director who had been a flier in World War I, and that the marriage was unraveling.

Jack and "Inga-Binga" — his pet name for her — lived together in the capital, and he even considered marrying her. The affair and Jack's intentions soon came to the attention of his father, who hit the ceiling.

"Damn it, Jack!" he bellowed. "She's already married!"

Apart from the F.B.I. surveillance, which Joe knew nothing about either, a scandal would surely erupt if there was a messy divorce, followed by marriage to the son of the ambassador. Joe wanted to avoid this at all costs.

On a weekend when he was off duty, Jack invited Inga to the Cape. Joe continued to upbraid his son about the relationship, but at the same time was not impervious to her Nordic beauty. Arvad's son Ronald said his mother thought Joe was "awfully hard, a really mean man."

And an amorous one. One weekend at the Cape, Ronald said, old Joe tried to "hop in the sack" with Inga. "She thought it was a totally amoral situation, that there was something incestuous about the whole family."

Naval intelligence officers were treated to the sounds of Jack and Inga-Binga in bed, recorded by the F.B.I. They came to the conclusion that the intelligence division was no place for the young ensign, if indeed he should be allowed to remain in the navy at all. Captain Howard Kingman, assistant director of the Office of Naval Intelligence, wanted to boot him out of the service, but fortunately for Jack, he was overruled.

On January 15, 1942, he was reassigned to the Charleston post, where he seethed in rebellion — and boredom. Joan and Clay Blair, Jr., in an interview with Inga's son, discovered that even in his exile Jack continued to see Inga-Binga. "She used to go down and visit him," Ronald said. "And he would go AWOL and come up to Washington to visit her."

Finally, the affair ran out of steam. Inga went to Hollywood, where she married Tim McCoy, the cowboy star. She died at the age of sixty in 1973, and was remembered all her life by Jack Kennedy as his first truly passionate involvement.

Nothing ever surfaced to indicate that Inga was anything but loyal to the United States, but her file continued to repose in the F.B.I. archives. Jack, who later learned about the surveillance, was furious and remained so all his life.

When he was President, J.F.K. was invited to speak at Harvard's graduation ceremonies, where he met an industrialist who had once been an F.B.I. agent. His job: to keep a close watch on Inga Arvad. The man greeted Jack, who stared at him coldly and whispered, "You-son-of-a-bitch!"

In Charleston, Jack's job was even more frustrating than it had been in Washington. He wanted action, but all he got were assignments to travel to defense plants to instruct workers on basic protection against enemy bombing attacks.

As President, J.F.K. was rarely stumped by a question — his encyclopedic mind absorbed information like blotting paper. But as a naval officer lecturing at factories, he proved somewhat less than all-knowing.

A short time after he arrived in Charleston, he completed a lengthy talk at a plant that included all the steps to take if the Nazis should suddenly loose their bombs on the premises. At the conclusion, a worker raised his hand and asked, "Suppose we get hit by an incendiary bomb that doesn't go off. How do we go about defusing it?"

Jack looked blank. He hadn't the faintest idea. The navy manual he had studied for the lecture had said nothing about this eventuality. But he recovered quickly. "I'm glad you asked that question," he said brightly. "I'll have a bomb specialist come down next week and explain it."

Both Jack and Bobby, itching for active duty, had their father pull strings to get them combat assignments.

In 1945 Bobby was stationed at Harvard in a naval reserve program and was bored out of his mind. In mid-year he wrote happily to Jack: "Pappy has got some angle to get me out of college." Joe had put in a call to his old friend James Forrestal, Secretary of the Navy, and Bobby was transferred to a destroyer, the U.S.S. *Joseph P. Kennedy, Jr.*, in the Caribbean.

In 1942, Jack was facing a transfer from Charleston to the Panama Canal, which he feared would be even more boring than lecturing to war workers. Joe called Forrestal and Jack was sent instead to training school, then shipped out to the South Pacific.

He wrote home often, but about July the letters ceased abruptly.

Back at Hyannis Port, Rose remained close to the house, listening to the war news on the radio. On the morning of August 6, 1943, she was startled to hear that the navy had announced that "Lieutenant John Kennedy had been saved."

It was the first time she learned that her son had been missing in action in the Pacific. Unable to reach Joe, who had driven to Osterville, a few miles from the house, she kept the radio blaring, hoping to hear more.

Joe, however, had known. Four days earlier, he had been informed that Jack was missing, and nobody had to tell him the ominous implication of that word — missing often meant killed in action. Still, he had told no one until he could learn more.

He, too, listened constantly to the radio, and heard the brief announcement that Jack had been "saved." He whooped, lurched forward, and lost control of the car. The car bumped some thirty feet into a grassy field before he could brake to a stop.

Several days later, Rose and Joe were told that their son was an authentic war hero, having rescued the crew members of his PT boat after it had been sliced in two by a Japanese destroyer in the Solomon Islands. For his heroism, the Navy and Marine Corps Medal was pinned to his chest, beside his Purple Heart, in an outdoor ceremony at Chelsea Naval Hospital in Boston, where he had undergone spinal surgery.

The citation, signed by Admiral William F. "Bull" Halsey and reported in the June 12, 1944, *New York Times*, read:

> "For extremely heroic conduct as commanding officer of Motor Torpedo Boat 109 following the collision and sinking of that vessel in the Pacific war area on August 1–2. Unmindful of personal danger, Lieutenant Kennedy unhesitatingly braved the difficulties and hazards of darkness to direct rescue operations, swimming many hours to secure aid and food after he had succeeded in getting his crew ashore. His outstanding courage, endurance, and leadership contributed to the saving of several lives and were in keeping with the highest traditions of the United States Naval Service.

Years later, while Kennedy was campaigning for the Presidency in Ashland, Wisconsin, a young man asked him to describe the circumstances under which he became a war hero.

His succinct answer: "It was involuntary. They sank my boat."

One story, which has been unreported, of that adventure in the Solomons concerns the hero's daughter, Caroline.

First, the facts: After his boat had been sunk and two of his eleven-man crew killed, Lieutenant Kennedy and the others made their way to a tiny island where he hoped to signal a ship to rescue them. When none appeared, they swam to a second island, Nauru, where they were found by a group of natives. Jack picked up a coconut shell and, with his knife, scratched out a message: Eleven alive native knows posit and reefs nauru island kennedy."

Handing the shell to a native, he repeated over and over, "Rendova, Rendova," the base from which he had set out.

One nodded, saying "Rendova" to indicate he understood where he was supposed to take it. The natives delivered the shell to the island and late the next day another PT boat appeared to pick up the survivors. During his long ordeal, Kennedy suffered an injury to his already weakened back.

That coconut shell remained in John Kennedy's possession. After his election to the Presidency, he placed it on his desk along with carved ivory pieces, photos of his family, and other knick knacks.

Caroline learned the story before she was four. After his assassination, she continued to have an almost total recall of her White House years. David F. Powers, a friend, Presidential aide, and now curator at the J.F.K. library, learned this during an emotion-charged incident one day ten years after the murder in Dallas.

In 1973, the library, which now stands at Columbia Point, Boston, had not yet been built. All of J.F.K.'s personal belongings, including the objects from the Oval Office, were being stored in a temporary building in Waltham, Massachusetts.

That year, Jackie took Caroline and John, Jr., to view the memorabilia. John, then thirteen, did not remember any of it, but Caroline, wandering through the aisles, recognized everything. Carefully, she explained to a wide-eyed John what each thing was. And, of course, she spotted the coconut shell, knew its history, and related it to her brother.

Powers's eyes misted over as he told the story. "It was a remarkable experience. She was barely six years old when she last saw all those things, yet they were vividly in her mind."

The Tragedies Begin

The remainder of 1944 was bleak for the Kennedys.

In August, Joe, Jr., died while flying a mission over the English Channel. In September, Kathleen's new husband, the Marquess of Hartington, a captain in the Coldstream Guards, was killed while leading an infantry charge in Normandy.

Jack, awaiting a medical discharge, took a leave of absence from the hospital and went to the Cape, where his father was mourning the death of the nobleman with silent grief, isolating himself from family and friends, listening to somber symphonic music in his darkened bedroom. Jack, the older children, and their close friends buried their sorrow beneath a layer of boisterousness, raiding Joe's liquor supply, playing hard physical games, and singing noisily.

Once they were carrying on so loudly that Joe, eyes red-rimmed, yelled down from his bedroom window, "Jack, don't you and your friends have any respect for your dead brother?"

Jack did have respect and, despite their many conflicts, a great deal of love. The father had instilled a sense of family in him and the others that would never leave. While he was waiting for his discharge, Jack asked twenty family members and close friends of his brother's to write personal reminiscences. Contributions came in from Harold Laski, Honey Fitz, Ted Reardon and Robert Downs, Joe's Harvard classmates, Arthur Krock, John J. Daly, Joe's archrival in sailing races, and George Taylor, a black valet who had become a close friend at Cambridge. The result was the seventy-five-page book, *As We Remember Joe*, published privately by the Kennedys and sent to family and friends as a Christmas present in 1945. Only 500 copies were printed and these are now collector's items.

Teddy, then twelve, wrote a piece for the book and, refusing to accept his sister Eunice's advice to say "how wonderful and strong and calm Joe was," told it like it was:

"I recall the day the year before we went to England. It was in the summer and I asked Joe if I could race with him. He agreed to this so we started down to the pier about five minutes before the race.

"We had our sails up just as the gun went off for the start. This was the first race I had ever been in. We were going along very nicely until suddenly he told me to pull in the jib. I had no idea what he was talking about. He repeated the command in a little louder tone; meanwhile, we were slowly getting farther and farther away from the other boats. Joe suddenly leaped up and grabbed the jib. I was a little scared but suddenly he seized me by the pants and threw me into the cold water.

"I was scared to death practully. I then heard a splash and I felt his hand grab my shirt and he lifted me into the boat. We continued the race and came in second. On the way home from the pier he told me to be quiet about what happened in that afternoon. One fault Joe had was that he got very easily mad in a race, as you have witnessed. But he always meant well and was a very good sailor and swimmer."

Later Jack said, "It was one of the nicest things in the book."

Jack wrote a five-page essay, which included this tribute:

"It is the realization that the future held the promise of great accomplishments for Joe that made his death so particularly hard for those who knew him. His worldly success was so assured and inevitable that his death seems to have cut into the natural order of things. But at the same time there is a completeness to Joe's life, and that is that completeness of perfection. . . . And through it all he had a deep and abiding faith — he was never far from God — and so I cannot help but feel that on that August day, high in the summer skies, "death to him was less a setting forth than a returning."

He concluded with a quotation from the British novelist and poet, Maurice Baring, a devout Roman Catholic whose wit and unsinkable spirit were much like his brother's:

When spring shall wake the earth,
And quicken the scarred fields to new
  birth,
Our grief shall grow. For what can Spring
  renew
More fiercely for us than the need of you.

Jack made a gently humorous reference in the book to his old rivalry with his brother. In a foreword preceding his own contribution, he wrote: "My only hesitancy in collecting these essays was that I doubted that Joe, if he had a voice in it, would have approved. But I have disagreed with him before, so here they are."

For the remainder of his life, Joseph Kennedy, Sr., could not bring himself to read the memorial book. His eyes brimmed with tears each time he picked it up.

Kennedy was discharged from the navy on March 16, 1945. He never put in for a disability pension, though he was entitled to one, but retained his $10,000 G.I. insurance, later collected by Jackie. Like many veterans who had not embarked on careers before entering the service, he wondered what he would do with his life.

After a three-month rest in Arizona to recuperate still more from his spinal surgery, J.F.K. opted for a fling at journalism. In the cushy job his father arranged for him as a special Hearst correspondent, he went to San Francisco in April to cover the birth of the United Nations. Then he went to England for the 1945 elections on July 5, when

Winston Churchill was ousted from power by the Socialist Labor Party. Later that month he covered the Potsdam conference, where President Harry S Truman, Clement Attlee, the new British Prime Minister, and Premier Stalin of the U.S.S.R. clarified the agreements reached at Yalta. Few twenty-eight-year-old reporters drew such dream assignments without long apprenticeship on the police and other local beats.

It didn't take Jack long to find that, while journalism had a certain excitement, he preferred doing things rather than writing about others who did them. This discovery fit squarely into his father's long-range plans. Joe had programmed his eldest son for a political career, but now that he was gone, the mantle fell on Jack.

In 1957, Joe said proudly, "I got Jack into politics. I told him Joe was dead and that it was his responsibility to run for Congress. He didn't want to. He felt he didn't have the ability. But I told him he had to."

Jack admitted it was indeed Joe who propelled him into the political world. "It was like being drafted," he said. "My father wanted his eldest son in politics. 'Wanted' isn't the right word. He demanded it. You know my father."

And so Jack Kennedy's eighteen-year political career began.

Chapter Four

Politics and Jackie

In April, 1946, John Kennedy made his first political move. He announced his candidacy for the Democratic nomination to fill the seat about to be vacated by James M. Curley in the House of Representatives. Curley, who represented the Eleventh Congressional District, comprising Cambridge, part of Somerville, and four Boston wards, resigned to reclaim his job as mayor of Boston.

Defeating nine other candidates in that solidly Democratic district, Kennedy easily won the election in November, 1946, and a seat in the eightieth United States Congress. That year he was also selected by the United States Junior Chamber of Commerce as one of the ten most outstanding men of the year.

The new Congressman lived in a three-story house at 1528 Thirty-first Street in fashionable Georgetown. Eunice, who was working for the Justice Department, shared the quarters. He had an office, room 322, in the

Old House Office Building, and another in Boston in the Federal Building. With another freshman congressman, Richard M. Nixon, he was appointed to the House Education and Labor Committee.

In the spring of 1951, Charles Bartlett, a Washington-based journalist, introduced him to Jacqueline Lee Bouvier, the daughter of Janet Norton Lee and John Vernon Bouvier II, a wealthy and socially well-connected stockbroker. They began to date and were married the following year.

Then, after three terms in the House, Kennedy decided to oppose Henry Cabot Lodge, who had held the Massachusetts Senate seat for three terms, in the 1952 election. With his mother and his brothers and his sisters and the vast Kennedy machine behind him, Jack garnered 51.5 percent of the senatorial votes, even though the head of the ticket, Gen. Dwight D. Eisenhower, swept the state.

First Hurrah

At twenty-nine, he was tall and thin with hair that never stayed combed, high cheekbones, a square jaw, and a wide toothy smile, presentable enough to voters but hardly a dynamic personality. His oratorical gifts were minimal, his reedy voice and staccato manner of speaking would not mesmerize audiences. He knew, too, that the full scorn of his opponents would be directed at him because he was the grandson of two political leaders and the son of a wealthy former ambassador with limitless resources to finance a campaign. Moreover, even though his family's roots had been planted in Boston, Jack himself had grown up in New York, and by 1946 the only Bostonian he knew was his grandfather, Honey Fitz.

He didn't even have a home in the state, much less in the district. On the documents he filed to become a candidate, he listed as his residence the Hotel Bellevue near the gold-domed State House in Beacon Hill. Many Boston pols, including Honey Fitz, lived there. Later, Jack rented a dingy little apartment at 122 Bowdoin Street, which became his official residence, although he rarely occupied it.

The Eleventh District was an ideal launching pad because his mother had been born within its boundaries, and his grandfather, Honey Fitz, began his political career there. It was, and still is, Kennedy territory.

His first move was to enlist the help of Dave Powers, a war veteran who was looking for something to do. Dave, who lived in Charlestown, which was Ward Two of the district, knew every stevedore who worked on the waterfront, every factory worker, and almost every family. He told Jack to concentrate heavily on Charlestown because of its strongly Irish population and because one of his strongest opponents, John Cotter, was a native. "Win Charlestown," Dave said, "and you'll have a big advantage."

Dave told Jack that Charlestown's working-class population had basic life goals: jobs, a decent place to rear their families, and good educations for their children. Jack stressed these policies in his speeches, and also made sure he wouldn't be looked upon as a rich kid invading the neighborhood. So on campaign swings into the area, he told his chauffeur to leave the limousine home and take the day off. He took the subway to Charlestown.

Patrick J. "Patsy" Mulkern, a professional Boston pol, was also one of the first to train Jack in the techniques of successful campaigning. The first day Patsy met the young candidate, he noticed Jack was wearing sneakers.

"For the love of Christ," he told him, "take those off. You think you're going to play golf?" Patsy also ordered him to get rid of his pink shirt.

Jack complied.

Patsy had other advice. He counseled Jack to leave his Harvard classmates in Cambridge. "The guys with the big words," he explained, "might turn off voters."

Dave Powers had problems in his home community with critics who assailed Jack as a carpetbagger. Replying to them was a daily, often discouraging job. Kennedy told him to stand firm and that one day he would look back on those days and tell everyone with pride that he fought with Jack on Saint Crispin's Day. They were battling together, Kennedy said, "we few, we happy few, we band of brothers."

Powers admired the stirring words, thinking that young Jack had fine literary as well as political talents. Years later, he discovered that the line was from William Shakespeare. In *King Henry V*, the young monarch makes a galvanic address to his troops on the eve of the battle of Agincourt. The passage was a favorite of both John's and Bobby's.

In every campaign, charges that he was a silverspoon candidate trading on his family's wealth haunted Jack. The attacks were revived in 1961 when Ted Kennedy ran to fill his brother's unexpired Senate term.

The most famous of these was the savage assault hurled by his opponent for the Democratic nomination, Edward J. McCormack, the thirty-eight-year-old Attorney General of Massachusetts and favored nephew of Speaker of the House John W. McCormack. In the first of two debates, young McCormack dramatically pointed to

Ted, who was seated beside him on the stage at South Boston High School, and said in a shrill, angry voice, "You never worked for a living! You never ran for or held an elective office. We need a senator with experience, not arrogance, and the office of United States senator should be merited, not inherited."

Later, in his closing arguments, McCormack once again turned to Ted and charged, "I ask . . . that if his name were Edward Moore, with his qualifications — with your qualifications, Teddy — if it was Edward Moore, your candidacy would be a joke. And nobody is laughing because his name is not Edward Moore. It's Edward Moore Kennedy!"

Young Kennedy sat through the assault, his face drained of color. When the debate ended, he hurried from the building, flanked by his aides, without saying anything to friends or the press.

Ted faced many similar charges during the campaign, though none so public or so devastating. One day, while speaking to workers outside a factory, one heckler boomed out, "Hey, Kennedy! You never worked a day in your life!"

From the other side came a sympathetic response: "Never mind, Teddy. You haven't missed a thing."

Once Jack silenced a heckler at a rally with a terse one-liner. John Cotter's supporters were angry that Jack, the outsider, had come in to beat him in his own backyard.

When Jack rose to speak, a Cotter backer bellowed, "Hey, Kennedy! Where you from? New York? Palm Beach? Cape Cod?"

Kennedy stopped his speech, strode to the edge of the platform, and pointed a finger at the man. "No one asked me my address when I was on a PT boat in the Solomon Islands," he said, "and don't you forget it!" The crowd roared approval.

"The girls all went for him," Patsy Mulkern said. "That head of hair he had . . . Every girl thought she was going to be Mrs. Kennedy." In Lynn one day with the candidate, Patsy noticed a large crowd in the street in front of a clothing store. "There's some guy running for senator up there," the owner told him. Then he added, "I hope he keeps running forever. I've sold more gowns today."

The girls, Patsy said, were buying "hiring gowns," special outfits to wear when looking for a job. They were purchasing them in hopes that they might catch Jack Kennedy's eye. Every mother, Patsy said, was pushing her daughter, telling her, "Get up there and let him get a look at you. He might go for you."

Patsy and a colleague went to Hyannis Port after a heavy week of campaigning, during which Jack gave away a huge sum of money to charity.

"I was pretty hungry," Patsy said. "We didn't eat all afternoon. We got down to the cottage. We got in the kitchen, and I opened the ice box, and I was grabbing the peaches. I was doing a good job on the peaches when Jack came down.

"'What the hell are you doing?' he said.

"I said, 'What the hell do you think I'm doing? I'm eating.'"

" 'My peaches!' " Jack yelled.

"Jesus Christ," Patsy declared. "He's just given away a million dollars this morning and he's hollering about a few peaches!"

Patsy taught Jack that the shortest distance between a candidate and an important person whose help he was seeking was a simple telephone call. For months the Kennedys were trying to get Ben Butler, a leader in the Irish community who was cool to his candidacy, to get on their bandwagon.

"He had all the international lawyers and everybody else get hold of this Ben Butler," Patsy recalled. "So I got a hold of Jack one day by myself. I said, 'Let me tell you something, Jack. A ten-cent phone call can get him. . . . First you find out where he lives. Then you call him and meet him tomorrow at the Ritz for breakfast. And he'll be there.' "

Jack made the call and spoke to Butler, who, sure enough, showed up for breakfast at the Ritz. "Later on," Patsy said, "he thought Jack was the greatest guy who ever lived. He misjudged him, he said."

On one of their trips Jack told Patsy he played football at school. Patsy looked at his skinny frame and said, "What were you, the water boy?"

Patsy was convinced that if Jack lost the Senate race, he would never again run for public office. "He would never have taken a defeat and come back. Lots of fellows would, but not him. They want to be winners. They want to be first in everything. . . .

"The old gent [Joe, Sr.] was the same way. He grabbed this. Grab that. Grab this. What the hell, they *were* first, ain't they?"

Everyone in Boston knew that an Irish Catholic candidate would win the Irish Catholic vote, but a certain myopia toward bloc voting existed.

An election for shop steward was held at the Charlestown Navy Yard a short time before the primary. An employee of Swedish descent was opposing an Irishman. The navy yard had a total of 227 workers, only 3 of whom were Swedes.

After a brisk, brief campaign, the election was held and the Irishman buried his rival, 224–3. After he had accepted congratulations, the winner looked again at the vote count and remarked, "Those Swedes are a clannish bunch, aren't they?"

Jack may have had doubts about his chances of winning, but his grandfather's political foe, Jim Curley, had none. Curley was shown the names of the nine candidates and was asked who would take the race. Running his eyes down the list, he stopped at a name and put his finger on it.

"Kennedy?" he said. "How can he lose? He doesn't even need to campaign. He can go to Washington now and forget the primary and the election!"

However, the Kennedys took nothing for granted. Boston looked on in wonderment as family-style campaigning, never seen before, was launched. Dozens of Kennedy men and women descended on the city to canvass for votes, ringing doorbells, attending every function they could find, tirelessly working stores, factories, and business offices. Kennedy women talked about homes, children, and clothes with the wives. Kennedy men talked sports and politics with their husbands.

The Kennedy organization began neighborhood coffee and tea parties, at which family members, and often the candidate himself, appeared. Tons of cookies and gallons of beverages were fed to the residents, who were awed at meeting the now-famous family.

Jack, the rich kid, was self-deprecating in his talks and slowly tore down the wall of resentment raised when his candidacy was announced. Once he was asked to speak at a rally along with a number of candidates for the state legislature, each of whom was introduced as a boy from a low-income family who had "come up the hard way."

Kennedy, the last speaker, glanced at the others and confided to the audience, "I seem to be the only person here tonight who didn't come up the hard way." He received an ovation.

Dave Powers, though young in years, was as sharp as any of the older pols. When primary day dawned, he made certain that Kennedy men working at the polling stations were all wearing Eisenhower jackets so that there would be no doubt which candidate was favored by the vets.

The Eleventh was overwhelmed, and on June 18, Primary Day, his district gave him 22,183 votes. All nine opponents combined polled only 32,541. On Election Day, he swamped his G.O.P. opponent, Lester Brown, 69,000–26,000.

When Jack was elected, Grandfather Honey Fitz was eighty-three, yet still feisty, dapper, and able to talk on any topic at the rate of 200 words per minute. Throughout his mayoralty, Bostonians sang the jingle, "Honey Fitz can talk you blind on any subject you can find."

Once he went to Palm Beach with Rose and had such a grand time that for two days he forgot to stay in touch with his office. Someone said that perhaps the mayor had been swallowed up by a Florida alligator, a thought that was quickly refuted. "If Honey Fitz and an alligator had faced each other, you can bet it was the alligator that got stung," was the reply.

One of the few times Honey Fitz was at a loss for words occurred when his enemy, Jim Curley, saw him on the street corner holding a green flannel shoulder bag. He had been strolling with his grandson Ted, then about fifteen, who had come up from Milton Academy for the day and was carrying his books in the bag issued to all students. Ted had gone into a drugstore for a soda and had asked his grandfather to hold the bag for him.

When Curley walked past, he looked at Honey Fitz, stared pointedly at the bag, and said, as he swept by, "Still carrying your burglar's tools, aren't you?" Honey Fitz could only sputter in rage.

Honey Fitz's theme melody was "Sweet Adeline," which he sang any time he got a chance. On trips abroad he warbled it before crowned heads, and in Washington he sang it before Alfonso XIII of Spain and his queen. When F.D.R. went to South America, he visited one small city that boasted a large brass band. Honey Fitz had preceded Roosevelt to the continent and had sung his theme so often that the band was under the impression it was the national anthem of the United States. So when F.D.R. arrived, the band greeted him with the strains of "Sweet Adeline."

When his grandson was elected to Congress, Honey Fitz mounted a table at the victory party in a Boston hotel and, his high tenor voice still clear and sharp, sang "Sweet Adeline." John Kennedy applauded louder than anyone in the place.

"Those Damned Tea Parties"

John Kennedy's health problems worsened significantly after he entered Congress. In Europe on a fact-finding tour for the House Education and Labor Committee in 1947, he fell ill in London and was admitted to the London Clinic. His father's old friend, Lord Beaverbrook, sent his personal physician, Dr. Daniel Davis, to examine him. The results of his tests were frightening. Jack had Addison's Disease, and Dr. Davis believed he had only about one year to live. He was then thirty years old.

Addison's Disease is a serious disorder of the adrenal glands, first described by the English pathologist Thomas Addison in 1855. The ailment attacks the glands, on the upper portion of each kidney, which secrete adrenaline, hydrocortisone, aldosterone, and other life-sustaining hormones. When the cortex of the gland is affected, the secretions stop and bodily weakness ensues. Victims have bouts of extreme lassitude, little or no appetite, weight loss, and occasional spells of faintness.

Dr. Davis's diagnosis most probably explain the series of mysterious illnesses that began at Choate and continued intermittently for years.

Jack was lucky. The very year his condition was discovered researchers succeeded in making cortisone synthetically. Experiments showed that with daily doses of this artificial hormone, plus treatment with certain minerals to control loss of salt, patients could be kept in a state approaching normal health.

Transferred to the Lahey Clinic, in Boston, Jack was treated by a thyroid specialist and later by Dr. Janet Travell. His London illness and regular visits to Boston were explained by his office as treatments for "malaria," which he had picked up in the Solomon Islands during the war.

The malaria story was a cover-up. John Kennedy actually had a life-threatening disease controlled during his lifetime by daily shots of cortisone that replaced the hormones his adrenals could not supply. This was never admitted by the family or the White House.

The injections enabled him to function normally, which for John Kennedy was at a pace just short of frantic during his congressional term when he began eyeing a seat in the Senate or the governorship of Massachusetts.

In pursuit of one of these goals, he set up a heavy schedule, spending four days in Washington every week, then flying to Boston for three days of nonstop speech making around Boston and the rest of the state. Francis X. Morrissey, executive assistant in his Boston office, said that in the next four years only ten minutes were alloted for meals, which consisted of hamburgers and milk shakes. Morrissey estimated Kennedy visited 350 communities, talked to 1,000,000 people, and shook hands with 750,000 of them in that time.

When Jack finally made up his mind to wrest a Senate seat from the powerful incumbent, Henry Cabot Lodge, in 1952, he doubled his already murderous pace. His day began before dawn. He went anyplace he could find a potential vote: receptions, luncheons, teas, garden parties; he stood before banks, at textile mills, in shopping centers; he visited newspaper offices, veterans' headquarters, and even went into the holds of ships anchored in the Boston harbor to introduce himself to fishermen; he talked to businessmen at Kiwanis, Rotary Club, and Elks luncheons; he went to every college and most high schools in the state. He slept only three or four hours a night.

There were some hairy moments during these twenty-one-hour days. Once, en route to Boston from Cape Cod in a small plane, he looked up from a speech he was preparing to see tongues of fire behind him in the cabin. Swiftly, he grabbed a fire extinguisher and trained the nozzle on the flames. When they were doused, he went back to his speech.

The Kennedy campaign for the Senate was a marvel of efficiency and coordination. Planned in Joe Kennedy's Park Avenue offices in New York, it called for partitioning the entire state into units. In each town, village, or community, a "Kennedy secretary" would be named, usually a volunteer who would act as eyes and ears for headquarters. At strategy sessions, places where the candidate would appear during a swing around the state were selected, and calls would go out to the Kennedy aides there.

"We're coming to Pittsfield [or Northampton or Worcester] on the twelfth for three days of campaigning," the secretary would be told. "Start setting it up."

"It" meant sending headquarters lists of key places the candidate could visit: civic organizations, social centers, housing projects — everywhere potential voters could be found.

Headquarters dug up a vital bit of political information — there were more women voters than men in the state. Thus, the coffee and tea parties, begun in the 1946 race, were even more important now. Headquarters would instruct a secretary to find a willing hostess who would loan her home or garden for a few afternoon hours and agree to invite a few dozen friends. Once arranged, headquarters would send a car or truck with coffee, tea, cake and cookies — and paper cups on which was printed: "Coffee with the Kennedys."

Sometimes the candidate himself would appear at the parties, though more often he would be represented by a member of the family. From all across the country, the Kennedys converged on Massachusetts to help Jack. Eunice, Jean, and Pat were there for almost six months. Ethel, married only two years to Bobby and already pregnant with her second child, raced around with them, stopping only a short while to give birth to Joseph

Patrick on September 24, then returning to the campaign in a few days.

Rose, then sixty-two and still slender and darkly beautiful, was as energetic as any of her children. She performed brilliantly for Jack, though not at the coffees or teas. She was royalty and she knew it, more effective on a platform at meetings, rallies, and dinners than mingling with guests. She knew, too, that she should appear as a wealthy woman at affairs attended by persons of high social standing, but more down to earth before working-class people. Thus, she would change her dress in the car while being driven from the former to the latter.

In one night, Dave Powers recalls, she would cover her head with a babushka and talk to less-affluent women about child care, then head for a wealthier group, emerging from the car in a different dress and shoes and a mink jacket.

In greeting people, the Kennedys were adept at the "Irish Switch," a maneuver learned from Honey Fitz. It consists of shaking hands with one person, while simultaneously engaging another in enthusiastic conversation. Honey Fitz even managed to encompass a third, at whom he would beam silently.

Bobby, who was twenty-six and had graduated from the University of Virginia Law School only the year before, was recruited to be Jack's campaign manager. Unschooled in the ways of Massachusetts politics, abrasive and aggressive, he soon succeeded in offending almost everyone in the state's Democratic organization.

Typical was the time several pols came to Jack's headquarters and stood around swapping yarns about past campaigns. Bobby, who was dashing around at his customary high tempo, became irritated. Finally he said to them, "Here are some envelopes. You want to address them. Fine. Otherwise, wait outside."

Jack, who told the story, observed, "Every politician in Massachusetts was mad at Bobby, but you can't make an omelet without breaking the eggs."

The omelet was indeed superb. Bobby got rid of the deadwood on the staff, insisted on a seven-day work week for everyone, and whipped a lumbering machine into the best organization in the history of the state.

But he was a terrible speaker. One of his first political talks was brief and to the point. Shy, his hands trembling and his voice sounding strangled, he rose before a group of voters and said, "My brother Jack couldn't be here. My mother couldn't be here. My sister Eunice couldn't be here. My sister Patricia couldn't be here. My sister Jean couldn't be here. But if my brother Jack were here, he'd tell you Lodge has a very bad voting record. Thank you." And he sat down.

For relaxation during swings, Kennedy would often play Monopoly, the board game in which participants buy and sell expensive properties using stacks of paper money. Unlike his father, who wheeled and dealt successfully in real big bucks and properties, Jack was a frequent loser in his make-believe business enterprises.

John Kennedy discovered that not everyone in Massachusetts knew who he was or what office he was seeking. The historian James MacGregor Burns tells about the time J.F.K. was driving to Boston from Worcester, about an hour away, when he stopped at a diner for a chocolate milk shake. Atop the diner was a huge billboard with his name in giant-sized letters.

"Hello," Jack said to the owner as he was leaving, "I'm John Kennedy."

He was greeted by a blank stare and a questioning "Who?"

Kennedy, puzzled, answered, "John Kennedy, running for United States senator."

Little recognition. "John Kennedy," the man repeated. "And running for what?"

Jack gave up and walked out. The experience taught him that billboards alone wouldn't sway voters.

It was inevitable that the grueling pace of the campaign would cause his back condition to flare up. It was only half over when he began experiencing severe pains. Still, he kept on, mounting stairs to shake hands with voters even though one leg was dragging. He never complained of the pain, Morrissey recalled, but toward the close of the race he was forced to use crutches to get around.

In the final weeks, Rose decided to take a straw poll among taxi drivers. En route to her son's apartment on Beacon Hill, she asked a cabbie whom he favored. He told her "that young fellow Kennedy" would win.

Suddenly the driver, recalling that he was driving toward a well-known address in Beacon Hill, looked in the rearview mirror and asked, "You aren't by any chance related to him, are you?"

Proudly, Rose revealed her identity.

"Am I glad to see you!" the driver said. "Your son owes me a dollar sixty-five!"

Rose's straw poll began and ended that night.

Lodge watched the increasing success of the tea parties with dismay, and tried to ridicule them in his urbane sophisticated manner. In virtually every speech he made, he would say, "I am told these tea parties are quite pleasant little affairs, and I'm sure they are non-fattening."

He was wrong. They fattened up Kennedy's vote considerably. In its final tabulations, the Kennedy camp found that a total of 70,000 guests across the state had attended the gatherings. On Election Day, Jack defeated Lodge by 70,737 votes, even though President Eisenhower had made a special journey to Massachusetts to help the Republican candidate.

A coincidence? Lodge didn't think so. Asked why he thought he lost, his reply was somewhat less sophisticated than his early utterances: "It was those damned tea parties," he snapped.

The Senator Takes a Wife

At thirty-three, he still looked like a high-school kid. In the halls of Congress, he was sometimes mistaken for a page and asked to run errands, a fact that was embarrassing to him and the ones who asked.

One brisk fall afternoon in 1950, he was taken for a high-school student. Torby MacDonald, his Harvard roommate, was coaching the backfield at Medford High North of Cambridge and had invited Jack to work out with the team.

Dressed for football, Kennedy loped onto the field searching for Torby but was stopped by a first-string halfback who told him, "Hey, kid, come on over and snag some passes." For ten minutes, Jack ran up and down the field. Then he was assigned to catching punts and, finally, to tackling drill.

As he prepared for this, John Prior, the head coach, came by and asked the halfback, "Say, how's the new recruit doing?"

The boy shook his head. "I don't know, Coach," he said. "He's okay, but needs a lot of work. By the way, what year is he in?"

Prior identified the "recruit" as the United States congressman from the Eleventh District.

In Washington, a subway car shuttles all day long between the Senate Office Building and the Capitol. The journey, which takes only a few minutes, is free to tourists as well as officials. One day Kennedy stepped forward to board the shuttle, but a guard put out his arm to bar him. "Just a minute," the guard said. "Let the senators go first."

Like millions of other men, all three Kennedy brothers met their wives through fix-ups. Bobby's sister Jean, three years older than he, got him together with Ethel at a skiing party she arranged in 1947. Ten years later, Jean dragged a reluctant Joan Bennett from her dormitory to meet her brother Teddy. And Charles Bartlett, the *Chattanooga Times* columnist, acted as matchmaker for Jack and Jackie.

The first time he tried to introduce them was a flop. Bartlett had met her in East Hampton a number of times and felt that the British beaus who were flocking around "were not up to her," that Jack would be a perfect date and, perhaps husband.

"I did conceive the idea of introducing them really very early," he said. "My brother got married in 1948 and I can remember at that wedding in Long Island trying to get Jackie Bouvier across this great crowd over to meet John Kennedy. . . . I got her about halfway across and she got involved in a conversation with Gene Tunney [the former heavyweight boxing champion]. And by the time I got her across, he had left."

Two years later, Bartlett made another effort, which was only slightly more successful. He invited them to a small dinner party at his Georgetown home. "After the dinner," Bartlett recalled, "I walked her out to the car and Jack Kennedy came sort of trailing after and he was muttering shyly, 'Shall we go someplace and have a drink?'" At that moment, Jackie noticed that one of the other guests, who had preceded them out of the house, was in the car waiting for her, and so she politely declined Jack's invitation.

Jackie went to Europe, Jack became involved in his senatorial campaign, and, with both absent from Washington much of the time, Bartlett's plans appeared dashed. Moreover, in the spring of 1951, Jackie became engaged to John Husted, a young New York stockbroker and Social Registerite.

But by this time Bartlett's wife, Martha, had become involved, and if Charlie was ready to give up, she was not. One day, when she knew both Jack and Jackie were in the capital, she gave a dinner party. Knowing Jackie's fiancé was in New York, she urged her to invite the handsome young Kennedy. She did; he accepted. "This was the beginning of the serious courtship which went down to the priest," Bartlett said.

Jackie was working as inquiring photographer for the *Washington Times-Herald*. Between assignments, she and Jack Kennedy shared cozy dinners in small suburban restaurants, walked the streets of Georgetown, and held hands at the movies.

In the fall of that year, she ditched Husted, who suspected the move was coming, because her letters from Washington had become sporadic and painfully brief. The end came one day when she met him at an airport and dropped the sapphire-and-diamond ring he had given her into his jacket pocket.

Jack Kennedy, now nearing thirty-seven, was in love for the second time in his life. Jackie had a sensuousness about her that intrigued and aroused him; she was aloof and always very much the lady, yet he felt that the innocent-appearing exterior she showed to the world through her breathless voice and open-eyed expression masked a deeper river of passion and mystery.

In May, 1953, she went to London to cover the coronation of Queen Elizabeth II. Jack spent horrendous sums making transatlantic phone calls, during one of which he asked her to marry him. The connection was poor and Jackie's light voice was barely audible, but he heard her acceptance. On June 25, 1953, they became officially engaged.

The announcement would have been made sooner, but Paul F. Healy had written a major article about Kennedy that the *Saturday Evening Post* was about to publish on June 13. Its title: "Jack Kennedy — The Senate's Gay Young Bachelor." Not wanting to embarrass the magazine, and perhaps to rule himself out its pages forever, Jack asked that the announcement be held up for about a couple of weeks.

Nine days before the wedding, Jack and Jackie went to the Newport city hall to apply for a marriage license. Jack, in shorts and a sport shirt, was approached by a newspaper photographer who asked them to pose for a picture. Jack demurred; he wasn't dressed properly, he explained and, after all, he was a United States senator.

The photographer had an idea. Removing his own jacket, he loaned it to Jack. A young law student standing nearby offered his tie. Kennedy donned the coat, knotted the tie, combed his unruly hair, and stepped to the window to sign the license application. As he did so, the photographer snapped his picture from the waist up standing next to Jackie, who was wearing a summer print with a fitted bodice.

Next day, the paper's readers never knew that the conservatively garbed senator had actually looked outlandish in jacket, tie — and shorts.

Jack had two bachelor parties, one for 350 guests in Boston and another for just two dozen close friends in Newport. Hugh D. Auchincloss, the bride's stepfather, hosted the latter at the Clambake Club, a rambling wooden structure on Eadton Point overlooking Long Island Sound.

The club, founded in 1895, had a membership that consisted then, as it does now, of the highest strata of Newport society. "Hugh-dee" reserved the oak-paneled members' room and ordered an elegant dinner, to be served, of course, on expensive dishes with costly stemware.

Ruby S. Gray, the club's chef for twenty-eight years, who was then second cook, recalls that a five-foot statue of a lighthouse keeper, made of sugar, had been created by the kitchen staff and stood in the center of the table. Before the dinner was served — boiled lobster, clams casino, clam chowder with tiny fish balls, and corn bread, all Jack's favorites — Paul "Red" Fay suggested a royal toast to Jackie. (Fay, a friend from PT-boat days, later became Undersecretary of the Navy.)

A royal toast meant that the glasses from which it was drunk must never be used again. They must all be smashed against the fireplace. Jack agreed enthusiastically and, lifting his champagne-filled glass, offered the toast and then shattered it against the brick and stone. Everyone followed suit.

Auchincloss watched in dismay, his eyes on two dozen very expensive crystal glasses that lay in shards. Bravely, though, he asked the waiter for a new supply. When they arrived, Jack Kennedy, declaring himself overcome by his love for his bride-to-be, lifted his glass in a second toast. The company rose, drank — and followed Kennedy's lead in hurling the second set of glasses into the fireplace.

Hugh-dee had enough. The next set he ordered were ordinary kitchen glasses.

The guests didn't know it, but there were female eavesdroppers at the dinner. Ruby Gray recalls that about ten of Jackie's bridesmaids, in sneakers, silently invaded the club grounds to peer through the windows to see — and hear — what was going on.

Jack Kennedy told George A. Smathers, then senator from Florida and one of his ushers, that Jackie was the most beautiful bride he had ever seen.

She walked down the aisle of St. Mary's Roman Catholic Church in Newport, Rhode Island, stunning in an off-the-shoulder ivory silk taffeta gown with a portrait neckline, fitted bodice, and full skirt. Her veil, of rosepoint lace, was an heirloom that had been worn by her grandmother, Mrs. John Vernon Bouvier. Hanging from a lace-and-orange-blossom-tiara, it flowed behind her in a long train. Encircling her neck was a short, single strand of pearls, and she carried a bouquet of pink and white spray orchids and gardenias.

Kennedy, in striped trousers and cutaway, a white handkerchief peeping from a breast pocket, and a white carnation pinned to his left lapel, made a handsome groom — a barber had come up by plane from Manhattan to cut his hair. But his face bore fresh scratches from a headlong tumble he had taken into a thorny patch of wild roses during a touch-football game the day before on the 300-acre estate of his bride's parents.

The wedding, on September 12, 1953, was the most celebrity-studded affair Newport had seen in years. Some 800 guests jammed into the 550-seat church. Socialites and political notables who attended included House Speaker Joseph W. Martin, Jr., Governor Dennis E. Roberts of Rhode Island, three United States senators, ten people from the House of Representatives, and a large assortment of foreign dignitaries.

Marion Davies, who had been William Randolph Hearst's longtime mistress, was there, along with some of the country's most important business tycoons. Also present was the congressman who was elected to Jack's Eleventh District in

Boston when he moved to the Senate — Thomas P. (Tip) O'Neill.

The couple was wed by the Most Reverend Richard J. Cushing, archbishop of Boston, who was later elevated to cardinal, and a special blessing was read from Pope Pius XII.

Cardinal Cushing was a close friend of the Kennedys through the years. Rose, a devout Catholic and daily communicant, would talk to him endlessly each time they met. Cushing loved Rose but her garrulousness often bored him.

One time the two were scheduled to appear at a Boston function, and prior to their appearance they were asked to stay backstage in a small office until they were called. The cardinal, in his flat Bostonian accent, told a friend, "So there I was, in that little room with Rose Kennedy for a whole fah-ty five minutes, and believe me, that's no bah-gain!"

The next day, the newspapers reported that the bride was given away by Auchincloss because of the "illness" of her father. Auchincloss, a Social Registerite, had married Jackie's mother, Janet, after her divorce from John "Black Jack" Bouvier became final in 1938.

Actually, Black Jack — given the nickname because of his dark complexion, which he made even darker under the sun and sun lamp — was lying drunk in his hotel room at the Viking Hotel in Newport.

Bouvier, a stockbroker, had been beset by financial difficulties years before. A heavy drinker, he had begun imbibing the night before the wedding, and by mid-morning, when it came time to dress for the ceremony, he was lying across his bed in a drunken stupor.

Word was rushed to Janet, who, nervous enough by this time, verged on the panic state. Her husband was drafted as a substitute.

When he awoke, Bouvier was humiliated. For weeks thereafter, he would not emerge from his apartment on Manhattan's east side, drinking himself into oblivion daily. Four years later he was dead.

At Hammersmith Farm, the receiving line took two hours to snake past the newlyweds. After Jackie tossed her bridal bouquet, she changed into a gray suit and she and her husband drove to the Waldorf in Manhattan, where they spent their wedding night in a lavish suite. The next day they left for a two-week honeymoon in Acapulco and at the end of September returned to Washington to begin married life.

Chapter Five

Winning the Big Prize

On January 3, 1953, Jack Kennedy was escorted to the well of the Senate chamber by Leverett Saltonstall, the senior senator from Massachusetts, to be sworn in, then went to the last row of the Democratic section to take his seat. His office, a suite of four rooms on the third floor of the Senate Office Building, was across the hall from that of Richard M. Nixon, the new freshman senator from California.

Kennedy was appointed to the Senate Labor Committee, where he had the lowest seniority after five other Democrats and seven Republicans, and the Government Operations Committee, where his brother Bobby was an assistant counsel. Like other first-term senators, he applied himself mainly to regional issues in Massachusetts and New England.

Two spinal operations, one of which almost cost him his life, were performed in 1954 and 1955. During his hospital stay and convalescence following the second

103

surgery, he wrote Profiles in Courage, *biographies of U.S. lawmakers who had exhibited rare political bravery despite popular disapproval. Published in 1956, it won the Pulitzer Prize the following year.*

His political star also began to shine in 1956 when he nominated Adlai E. Stevenson to be the Democratic candidate for President of the United States. Kennedy adherents made a bid to have him nominated for Vice-President on the ticket, but he lost in a close race with Estes Kefauver of Tennessee.

Kennedy campaigned for Stevenson's election that fall. With an eye on the 1960 Presidental nomination for himself, he dispatched Bobby to travel with Stevenson and observe his campaign.

In 1958 he was reelected to his Senate seat by 874,000 votes. He continued to speak all over the nation and his popularity was rising. Often he was introduced as the "next President of the United States." Polls showed him leading all the other Democratic candidates and even some of the Republicans.

By then Steven E. Smith, Jean Kennedy's husband, had opened an "unofficial" campaign office and contacts were being made in all the states. On January 2, 1960, Jack Kennedy announced that he would be a candidate for the Democratic Party nomination. Then, convinced that the way to capture the nomination was to come to the convention armed with delegates, he entered seven primaries and won them all.

In August he won the party nomination in Los Angeles, and in November he was elected President.

Young Senator Kennedy

The Kennedys lived in several small rented homes in quiet and quaint Georgetown, only a mile from downtown Washington. Once the commercial center of the lower Potomac, Georgetown was one of the most prestigious, and expensive, residential areas in the capital.

For two years, between 1953 and 1954, they lived quietly. Jackie took courses in American history at Georgetown University and Jack took up painting as a hobby to relieve the tensions of his senatorial duties. In the evening, after Jack returned from the office and there were no special engagements, they would clip newspaper and magazine articles about themselves and paste them in a scrapbook.

They hunted for films they both wanted to see and stood in line to buy tickets, rarely bothered by autograph seekers. Jackie usually wore slacks, Jack a sweater. Occasionally, he would come home, announce that a couple of tickets were waiting for them at a Broadway box office, and the next day they would board a shuttle flight to New York.

Their favorite of favorites was *Camelot*, the Alan Jay Lerner-Frederick Loewe musical about the Arthurian legend. After seeing it, they bought the record and the tapes and played them often, even years later at 1600 Pennsylvania Avenue.

The passage Kennedy loved best came at the end, when King Arthur sang about the "one brief shining moment" that once was Camelot. After his death, Jackie gave an interview to author and journalist Theodore White, in which she compared the three years of his Presidency to that brief, shining moment, and the name "Camelot" was affixed forever to the Kennedy years in Washington.

The marriage was only a few years old when a story circulated that serious disagreements had arisen and that the couple was heading for divorce court. Old Joe, according to rumor, concerned that a marital breakup could harm Jack's political career, offered Jackie $1,000,000 to remain wed.

When the report reached her ears, Jackie picked up the telephone and called Joe. "Cheapskate!" she chided him.

Jackie was the only one who could needle Joe and get away with it. Once she painted a watercolor picture for him depicting a swarm of his grandchildren on a beach, looking out toward the water. "You can't take it with you," the caption read. "Dad's got it all." Joe guffawed when he saw it.

Searching for an estate where they could raise a family, Jack and Jackie came upon a hundred and thirty-year-old Georgian home on Chain Bridge Road in McLean, Virginia, only a half-hour drive from the city. Sitting on six and one-half acres of rolling countryside, well hidden from the road, it seemed ideal. Kennedy paid $125,000 for the place — called Hickory Hill — and Jackie began decorating it and preparing an elaborate nursery for the babies she hoped to have.

After the 1956 convention, when Jack lost the nomination for Vice-President, the young couple separated. He flew to his father's home on the French Riviera for a brief rest, while she went to Hammersmith Farm, her parents' estate in Newport. On August 23, a drama began that almost cost Jackie her life.

Her baby wasn't due until late September, but pain and hemorrhaging began and an emergency Cesarian was performed at Newport Hospital. The baby, a girl, was born dead and Jackie was greatly weakened by her ordeal. Kennedy, on a yacht in the Mediterranean, was unaware of the events until he returned to Val-sur-Mer. He flew home to be at her side, and when she had recovered they returned to Hickory Hill.

When Jackie entered the lovely nursery, she broke down in tears. Unable to remain in the house where her dreams of rearing a family had exploded, depressed by the bigness and loneliness of the home and grounds, she wanted to return to Georgetown. J.F.K. sold Hickory Hill to Bobby and Ethel, who by then had five children, for the $125,000 he had paid originally, and he and Jackie moved into a small furnished house at 2808 P Street.

Kennedy's first daughter, who died before baptism, and therefore was not named, now lies beside him on the grassy hillside of Arlington National Cemetery. The small plaque marking her resting place reads: "Baby Kennedy."

Caroline was born on November 27, 1957, while the young couple was living on P Street in Georgetown. She had a room of her own and there was no trouble housing her in the Big House at Hyannis Port. The Palm Beach home was another matter. There space was limited, and there was never enough room for the Kennedys, who would come and go without advance notice.

When Caroline was still an infant, Jack and Jackie flew down there for a brief vacation, but Teddy was occupying the room they expected to have. He was planning to leave the day they arrived, but he hadn't told the housekeeper when he would vacate the premises.

Jack wasn't about to keep his little family in the hall while his brother made up his mind. When Teddy returned to the house he found that he had been evicted. All his belongings were stacked outside the room in the hallway; Jack and Jackie and Caroline were inside.

"I'd rather be dead than spend my life on these things," Kennedy said in 1954, pointing to a pair of crutches he had just leaned against a wall as he eased into a chair. He had suffered back pains ever since prep-school days when a disk in his back had herniated during a football scrimmage at Choate. It never healed completely, and the problem had worsened considerably in the Solomons after his ordeal in the water. Navy doctors had inserted a metal plate in his spine that left him in constant, often agonizing pain.

Thereafter he was on crutches much of the time, discarding them for public appearances. Like Franklin D. Roosevelt, whose disability was hidden because he was never photographed with braces on his useless legs, John Kennedy's crippling back problem was unknown to all but his close associates.

Two years after his election to the Senate, Kennedy made a major personal decision. An operation to fuse the vertebrae and insert another metal plate might relieve his acute distress, but he was warned that he could suffer fatal shock and infection because of his adrenal insufficiency. His chance of survival, doctors warned, was only fifty-fifty.

Rather than face the rest of his life in his crippled state, John Kennedy took the risk. On October 21, 1954, the operation was performed at the Hospital for Special Surgery on Manhattan's east side. It was a failure.

Twice during the next several weeks, doctors had to tell the Kennedys Jack was at the point of death from a severe infection, and twice a priest administered last rites. Jack recovered but the pains had not diminished. Four months later, after recuperating at Palm Beach, he underwent a second operation to remove the metal plate that left him with a three-inch hole in his back.

For the rest of his life, Kennedy was never completely free of pain, though there were times when it eased enough to allow him to sail, play golf, and even get into a game of touch football. He credited Dr. Janet Travell, later White House physician, with relieving much of the distress. She prescribed novocaine injections, lifts on his left shoe to minimize movements that strained the back muscles, and a rocking chair, which became a prominent part of the Oval Office and can still be seen at the Kennedy Library, south of Boston. J.F.K. also applied hot packs regularly, slept on a bed board, and wore a cloth brace.

When Jack was in the hospital for the second time, the film star Grace Kelly was visiting New York, where she dined with friends. Among the guests were Jackie and her sister, Lee. Later that year, Grace was to meet the bachelor Prince Rainier of Monaco, who would propose at a New Year's Eve party in the Kelly family's Philadelphia home.

Jackie and Lee, knowing Jack admired Grace for her cool beauty and elegance of manner in her movies, cooked up a scheme. Recalled Grace, "They asked me to go to the hospital with them to pay a visit and help cheer him up. They wanted me to go to his room and say I was the night nurse."

Grace demurred but the sisters insisted. They took her to the hospital, dressed her in a nurse's uniform, and practically pushed her into Jack's room. "I'm the new night nurse . . ." she began. But her Hollywood expertise couldn't help her pull it off. Jack Kennedy recognized her at once, and was delighted by her visit. "He couldn't have been sweeter or more quick to put me at ease," Grace said.

Kay Halle witnessed a remarkable demonstration of J.F.K.'s domination over pain. After he returned to work following his second back surgery, they met at a party in the Sulgrave Club in Washington. "He was leaning against the back of a chair," Halle recalled. "Someone was sitting in the chair, which had a high back, and he was leaning against the top. Suddenly the girl who was sitting in the chair got up, which meant that Jack went down, slid, and fell straight on the floor on the bottom of his spine. He turned white as a sheet, and I remember saying to him, 'Look, Jack, take both of my hands.'"

Kennedy demurred but finally rose with her help and continued the conversation, even though the pain had to be agonizing. "I was absolutely staggered," Halle said, "because when he landed I could hear his spine hit the floor. I thought that was the most remarkable demonstration of his iron courage and power to dominate the physical with his will."

Barry Goldwater, the Arizona Republican, had taken the floor in the Senate and launched into a lengthy harangue on a labor bill that had been introduced. It is customary for younger members to be assigned to preside at the duller and less-important sessions. Kennedy, who had a pressing dinner engagement at six P.M., had been asked to take the chair and was shuffling his feet impatiently as Goldwater droned on.

Time passed. The chamber slowly emptied until only a lone senator was left to hear the speaker. Kennedy looked at his watch. It was after six and

Goldwater was showing no sign of winding up. Finally Jack scribbled a note, called a page, and sent it to Goldwater, who paused and unfolded it.

"Must you always be such a shit?" Kennedy had written.

Goldwater burst into laughter and after a few moments ended his speech. Afterward he said, "I decided then I'd let him off. After all, he was in bad shape, so I finally sat down."

Kennedy's schedule was so overloaded that, inevitably, he missed some appointments. But, as he did at home when he was a child and as a preppie, he would charm his way out of trouble. "Everyone forgives him," said a close friend. "He gives them that big ingenuous grin, when actually he's about as ingenuous as an I.B.M. machine."

Teddy was a party boy. But Jack never was. Tip O'Neill recalled the time he attended a cocktail party at Ted's Georgetown home following the younger Kennedy's election to the Senate. The invitations specified that the festivities would begin at six P.M. and end at eight.

Tip, who had gone to several of Jack's parties, for which the invitations read the same, rose to go with the others at eight o'clock.

Ted was surprised. "Where you fellows going?" he asked. Reminded of the time limit on the invitations, he told them to forget it. "Besides," he said, pointing to the loaded tables, "we've got all that food." The company remained until mid-morning, eating, drinking, and spinning political yarns.

Jack was different. His guests left promptly at eight and he never stopped them.

Kay Halle remembers that as a representative and senator, Jack was rarely seen at the big Washington parties. When he did attend, he would sit off in a corner "with some congressman, senator, ambassador, or expert in a certain field," Halle said. She added, "He wasn't shy, he was reserved."

Jack Kennedy loved his father but came to disagree with him on nearly everything. Once he said, "There isn't a motive in him which I respect except love of family, and sometimes I think that's just pride." Soon after he entered the Senate, Jack told Lawrence H. Fuchs, chairman of the American Studies Department at Brandeis University, "My father is to the right of Herbert Hoover. He is absolutely predictable on every political issue. We disagree on almost everything."

At the same time, he was a son, and the ideological conflict troubled him. He wanted to know how other sons felt about their fathers. "Do you agree with everything in which your father believes?" he pressed Dr. Fuchs. When the latter replied that he did not, Kennedy asked, "Do you love your father?"

Recounting the incident, Dr. Fuchs said, "His point was that he had strong family loyalty and politics did not interfere with that. He was trying to say he wasn't going to back away from his closeness to his father. They cared about each other and he accepted his father's strong support for the Presidency for the good it could do him, but also because he loved his old man."

Several times, old Joe tried to pressure his son into voting on measures he favored, but Jack refused.

Once, when he was a Congressman, father and son attended a cocktail party at the home of Drew Pearson, the political columnist. A bill was being debated in the House and Joe was convinced his son was going to vote the wrong way. In the garden, Joe, Jack, and Kay Halle were discussing the measure. Joe turned to Kay and said, "I think Jack is making a terrible mistake."

J.F.K. quickly told his father, "Now look here, Dad. You have your political views and I have mine. I'm going to vote exactly the way I feel I must vote on this. I've great respect for you, but when it comes to voting, I'm voting my way."

On another occasion the patriarch was supporting Senate confirmation of Admiral Lewis Straus, who had been nominated as Secretary of Commerce by President Eisenhower. Joe asked his son to vote for Straus, an old friend, but Jack, who needed to establish liberal credentials for the Presidential race he was planning, refused. He felt Straus had bungled his job as chairman of the Atomic Energy Commission and voted against his confirmation.

Loyalty to family was to blame for Jack's biggest blunder during his Senate years — the way he mishandled his vote on the censure of Wisconsin Senator Joseph R. McCarthy in 1954. McCarthy, who had shaken the nation by his anti-communist crusade in the early 1950s, was charged with un-ethical behavior that "tended to bring the Senate into dishonor and disrepute."

Every Democrat but one voted for censure. The single exception was John F. Kennedy.

Joe had nothing to do with his son's action. He said nothing, did nothing. Yet, paradoxically, he was mainly responsible. Joe McCarthy was a good friend of Joe Kennedy's, a frequent guest at Hyannis Port and Palm Beach, and at one time had even dated Jack's sister Pat. Joe had contributed money to McCarthy's Senate campaign, cementing the relationship. In 1952, when McCarthy was riding high, he could have gone into Massachusetts and done major damage to J.F.K.'s race against Lodge in heavily Catholic Massachusetts. Joe, aware that McCarthy with his communist issue had helped defeat Senator Millard Tydings in Maryland and Scott Lucas in Illinois, pleaded with him to stay out of Massachusetts.

Out of friendship, McCarthy agreed, and Jack knew that he owed him a considerable debt.

The vote for censure — the actual word in the language of the resolution was "condemn" — was 67–22. Along with Senator Alexander Wiley of Wisconsin, Kennedy was recorded as "not present and not announced."

Later, Jack offered a weak explanation, pointing out that in December, when the vote was taken, he was seriously ill following his back surgery. Senators must be present in the chamber for their votes to count, but he could have made his views public or exercised his privilege of "pairing" with another absentee senator, as his friend George Smathers did. Smathers, favoring censure, was paired with Homer Capehart of Indiana. (In pairing, an absentee senator enters into a voluntary agreement with another senator who intends to cast an opposing vote. The second senator may or may not be in the chamber, but the votes are not counted in the final tabulation, although each legislator's views are, of course, made public.)

In the end, Kennedy, torn by conflicting emotions, could not bring himself to vote for the censure of the man who was such a close friend of his father's and, in 1951, godfather of Bobby's first child, Kathleen.

The monumental irony of having written *Profiles in Courage* the year after he ducked the censure vote was not lost on Jack Kennedy. "I didn't have a chapter in the book about myself," he said wryly.

And he never managed to live down his nonaction. Five years after the vote, when he was campaigning in Wisconsin for the Presidency, he smiled weakly and slumped a little in his seat as reporters at a Gridiron Dinner sang to the tune of "My Darling Clementine":

> Where were you, John
> Where were you, John,
> When the Senate censured Joe? . . .

Jack's campaign to win the Vice-Presidential nomination in Chicago in that hot summer of 1956 was one of the briefest ever conducted. "It was an overnight affair," Hale Boggs declared. One of his visits that single day was to the hotel suite of Earl Long, then governor of Louisiana, who called himself "the last of the red-hot papas."

Social amenities meant nothing to Long. When Kennedy entered the suite, the governor greeted him in his B.V.D.'s, one-piece underwear that Long wore all his life. Kennedy gaped. He gaped still more when Earl Long, totally lacking in inhibitions, decided to polish his false teeth. As Jack watched, he removed the plates and rubbed and polished them until they gleamed, all the while talking politics to his visitor.

Despite its bizarre aspects, the visit was successful. Louisiana voted for Kennedy.

Kennedy was invited to Louisiana to campaign for the Stevenson-Kefauver ticket. Riding with Representative Hale Boggs, the Democratic whip, Kennedy was greeted by cheering throngs everywhere he went.

"I'd look around," Boggs recalled, "and he'd be pulling up his gray woolen socks. I said to him, 'Look, either wave at the people or quit pulling those socks up, and the next time you come down here, for God's sake get yourself a pair of garters or something! You can't ride around here with all these people and spend half your time pulling up your socks!"

"Until the day he died," Boggs said, "when I used to see him, he had the same kind of gray socks on, and he would pull them up all the time. It was one way he got rid of tension."

Going for It

Kennedy had three reasons for wanting to be President. He stated them frankly and clearly in 1958 at a dinner party in the home of journalist Joseph Alsop. Katherine Graham, now publisher of the *Washington Post* and *Newsweek*, recalled that evening when she, her late husband, Philip, Alice Longworth Roosevelt, and Kennedy had remained to talk after the other guests had gone.

Philip Graham turned to Kennedy. "Jack," he said, "you look awfully good. I'm sure you will be President someday, but I think you are too young to run now [he was forty-one] and I hope you don't."

Kennedy replied, "Well, Phil, I'm sorry but I'm running. There are three reasons: One is that I'm better than any other of the possible candidates except Lyndon Johnson. The second reason is that if I didn't run now, somebody else would run and be in the Oval Office for eight years, and probably dictate his successor. The third reason is that if I stayed eight years in the Senate intending to run, I'd end up being a lousy senator and a lousy candidate."

Old Joe's early teaching that winning was all that mattered took root in Jack. To Jack Bell, an Associated Press correspondent who analyzed J.F.K.'s chances for the Presidency in 1960, Jack wrote:

"You're correct about almost everything you write except one thing. You keep saying that, of course, Kennedy will end up as the Vice-Presidential nominee.

"I wish you'd get those goddamned words out of your typewriter because I'm never going to take second place!"

By 1958, a Kennedy-for-President boom was spreading around the country. Jack, responding to dozens of requests for speeches, was hitting the key voting areas, gathering enthusiastic suppport wherever he went. Autograph seekers came at him in waves, young girls sent him messages of undying love, and older Americans were captivated by his boyish good looks, flashing smile, and the sense he made in his talks. The media, seeing all this, helped his cause with cover stories (*Time*); analyses of his chances (*The New York Times Magazine*, *New Republic*, and *U.S. News and World Report*); a discussion of the rise of the brothers Kennedy (*Look*); and many feature articles in women's magazines. Few days passed without lengthy articles in the newspapers.

His office, said historian James MacGregor Burns, was like "a five-ring circus." People bustled in and out constantly; clerks and secretaries were never able to catch up with the mountainous paper work; aides wrote parts of speeches, arranged for his appearances, and fought to get the senator's attention.

Jack was the busiest in the suite, never still, a phone at his ear all day long, often talking to a distant part of the country and a visitor at the same time. Then he'd race out to keep an appointment.

He made every moment count, sometimes dictating while taking a bath in the morning. After a quick breakfast, he would bolt out of the house and drive himself to his office, often too fast.

Theodore C. Sorensen, his administrative assistant, was at the house one day for an early morning conference, then got into Jack's station wagon for the short drive to the Senate Office Building. Jack, at the wheel, passed a vehicle and moved ahead at a speed exceeding the posted limit.

Unfortunately, he had passed a police car. Waved to a stop, he was asked for his license and registration, neither of which he had. The cop, who did not recognize him, was about to take him to the station house to be booked when Sorensen intervened. Walking to the police car, he told the officer that the driver was John Kennedy, United States senator from Massachusetts.

"Why didn't he say so?" the cop asked, and went over to look. This time he recognized Jack and told him to get along. Sorensen drove the rest of the way.

Always running late, Kennedy frequently found he did not have enough time to catch a plane. Refusing to ask an airline to delay the flight, he would tell his chauffeur, John L. "Muggsy" O'Leary, to move over and he would take the wheel, driving to the airport at a dangerously high speed. O'Leary, knowing the way his boss drove, insisted on sitting in the rear instead of the "death seat" next to Kennedy.

Sorensen, who accompanied Jack on many of these wild dashes, agreed to sit in front. "Only," he explained, "for fear that, if I were in the backseat, the senator would turn around as he drove."

John Kennedy had a sharp mind, but there were times when, like everyone else, he blundered.

In San Antonio he delivered a brief address at the Alamo, the "cradle of Texas liberty" where all of the besieged heroic defenders of the fortified structure were killed when they refused Santa Anna's demand to surrender. After his talk, Kennedy glanced at his watch and saw he was running late.

Turning to Maury Maverick, a descendant of the famous Maverick family of Texas, he whispered that he'd like to slip out instead of remaining through the entire program. "Is there a back door?" he asked.

Maverick turned to him and stared. "Hell, Senator," he said, "if there had been a back door, there never would have been an Alamo!"

John Kennedy announced his candidacy on January 2, 1960, but clever snooping by a United Press International newsman discovered his intentions two weeks earlier, causing a furor in the Kennedy camp.

Wandering through Jack's office, the reporter picked up one of thousands of letters that were being prepared for mailing to key backers around the nation, saying Kennedy had made up his mind to make the race. "I am announcing on January 2 my candidacy for the Democratic Presidential nomination," it began. The reporter left with a copy and the next day the story was front-page news.

Pierre Salinger, Jack's press secretary, asked by other newsmen to confirm the story, made a weak excuse. "Kennedy was still undecided," he said, adding that the letter was just one of many drafts being prepared to cover "all possible eventualities" concerning the senator's decision.

"I have grave doubts the senator has even seen it," Salinger said.

Commenting on the leak and Pierre's explanation, one newspaper observed that it had equally "grave doubts" that Salinger would remain in his job for long.

Kennedy did announce his candidacy on January 2 in the ornate, high-ceilinged Senate Caucus Room, where, six years earlier, the Army-McCarthy hearings had enthralled the nation and immediately launched on the grueling primary campaigns in New Hampshire, Wisconsin, West Virginia, Indiana, and Oregon.

He was convinced he would win the nomination and then the grand prize. Soon after the announcement, he flew to Hyannis Port for a fundraising event. One of his neighbors asked him if he truly wanted to be President.

He replied, "I not only goddamn want to be President, but I goddamn will be President.

J.F.K. was good at subduing hecklers. During a speech in Wisconsin a leather-lunged man in the audience yelled, "Kennedy, I hear that your dad has offered only two dollars a vote. With all your dough, can't you do better than that?"

Jack won the crowd with his swift response. "You know that statement is false. It's sad that the only thing you have to offer is your vote and you're willing to sell that."

Listening to Jack's speeches, Rose decided his diction needed improving. So she wrote to him suggesting he practice these tongue-twisters: "Fanny Finch fried five floundering fish for Frances Fowler's father," and "Tie twine to three tree twigs." She assured him he'd get results in no time.

Jack had just finished a speech while standing on the rear platform of his campaign train when signals became mixed and the engineer began pulling away. A number of journalists, who hadn't expected the sudden departure, were outside in front of the crowd and were left stranded.

Kennedy grinned at them and waved. "Don't forget to write," he called out.

His most quoted quip during the campaign came when he responded to criticism that his wealthy father was spending vast sums to elect his son. He pulled out a telegram he said he had just received from Joe and read it with a straight face: "Jack, don't buy a single vote more than is necessary. I'll be damned if I'm going to pay for a landslide."

Kennedy was accustomed to newspaper criticism even on relatively minor issues, but he was rendered speechless one evening in Oshkosh, Wisconsin, by the nit-picking of a correspondent from *The New York Times*.

Earlier, the candidate had quoted a jingle written by playwright Robert E. Sherwood when F.D.R. was inaugurated:

> Plodding feet
> Tramp — tramp
> The Grand Old Party's
> Breaking camp.
> Blare of bugles
> Din — din
> The New Deal is moving in.

Just as the New Deal replaced Herbert Hoover's administration, which did little to ease the nation's plight during the Great Depression, Kennedy wanted to make the point that a change was needed after the Eisenhower years.

In his hotel lounge after the speech, Jack was approached by the *Times* man, who complained that the poem wasn't quite right. "What do you mean?" Kennedy asked.

The reporter explained that there was something lacking in the lines of the poem: "Blare of bugles / din — din."

"There should be another 'din' in there," he said. "'The blare of bugles, din — din — din.'"

Kennedy turned away and strode to the elevator. The next morning he groused to Dave Powers,

"Haven't we got enough troubles without that fellow complaining because he thinks there ought to be another din?"

In Detroit, a bowling team from the Knights of Columbus called Kennedy's hotel and asked if he had time for the members to come up for a hello and a handshake. His schedule was too pressing and he asked an aide to make an excuse for him.

"Tell them I've gone out," he said. "If I don't have their votes, I might as well give up."

Kennedy was perplexed by the Jekyll-and-Hyde attitude of Oregon's maverick senator, Wayne Morse, who had been all honey and smiles toward him earlier at a Jefferson Day dinner. Back at his hotel, he told Arthur M. Schlesinger, Jr., the historian who had delivered a talk at the dinner, "Half the time Wayne claps me on the shoulder and congratulates me; the other half, he denounces me as a traitor to liberalism and an enemy of the working class. It all reminds me of *City Limits* and the millionaire who, when he is drunk, loads Charlie Chaplin with gifts and insists that he spend the night, but, when he is sober, can't recognize him and throws him out."

Most analysts agree that Bobby's help was critical. Polly Fitzgerald, a Kennedy cousin by marriage who worked in every one of Jack's campaigns from 1946 on, recalled, "I saw Bobby get up in a snowstorm at six in the morning and thumb his way to a meeting of twenty-five people. I went with him to visit an elderly couple who had asked to meet him. Their name was Kennedy. He was sweet and gentle to them. It was a cherished moment in the frantic pace of campaigning.

"We walked through the railroad stations carrying our own bags. He would look at me and laugh and say, 'Aren't you glad that you married our cousin?' I bought him soup from machines in airline terminals and he bought us candy bars when dinner was impossible. I saw him run and swoop up two children afraid to ascend an escalator. I watched his rapport with the people at the organizational meetings — women came to work for Jack Kennedy, their hero — and when they met his brother they showed him pictures of their children and asked him about his. These were the days that were 'the making of the President.'"

Bobby was everywhere, whipping the organization to greater efforts, prodding, encouraging, offering innovative ideas.

"There was no question who was in charge," declared John English, a Long Island Democratic Party leader who worked closely with the brothers. "Bobby worked hard and kept a lot of different things going. There was a finance group, a citizens' group, people who wrote and distributed all kinds of literature. He directed them all and knew every moment who was doing what.

"He was his brother's surrogate. When Bobby spoke, everyone in the campaign organization from the most powerful political leaders on down listened.

"If you looked at the campaign, it was flawless. It was truly, as many have written, a 'well-oiled

Kennedy machine.' But it did not come about automatically. It took hard, hard work, and Bobby was responsible for much of the flawlessness."

Bobby was so good at his job that talk arose that he might be an even more attractive nominee than Jack. An attorney from California wrote just that to the senator, saying he should step aside and make way for his younger brother.

Jack replied, "This is to acknowledge your letter and to tell you that I am taking your recommendation under advisement. I have consulted Bobby about it, and, to my dismay, your idea appealed to him."

Jack's eye was always roving, even during hectic swings through dense, cheering throngs. In April, campaigning in Charleston, West Virginia, he was working the crowd in front of a large department store, shaking hundreds of hands, smiling and greeting everyone. Yet he still was able to notice an attractive woman standing to one side.

"Hey!" he said to Charles Peters, campaign manager in the area. "Let's move over to that blonde over there."

Peters looked and told him, "Hey, Senator, that's my wife!"

"We both laughed," Peters remembered. He added, "It was always prudent to keep her some distance from John Kennedy, because that was not his good side."

Kennedy was nominated on the first ballot at the Sports Arena Convention Hall in Los Angeles on July 13 that year. Insisting on being near the action, yet secluded from the convention chaos, he asked his aides to find him a hideaway. A perfect one was located — or so the staff thought. It was a three-bedroom penthouse apartment owned by the actor Jack Haley. The house had a hidden driveway where Jack's car could be secreted and was only a ten-minute drive from the Sports Arena Convention Hall.

The day Jack won, the media discovered his whereabouts, and soon the house on North Rossmore Avenue was swarming with TV people and their huge equipment trucks and scores of print journalists.

Jack looked out his window and remarked dryly to Dave Powers, who had scoured L.A. for the place, "This is one heck of a hideaway, isn't it?"

After winning the nomination, Kennedy accepted an invitation to appear on "Meet the Press," a weekly current-affairs program presided over by its creator, Lawrence Spivak. Kennedy was well aware that Spivak, the moderator, was a tough questioner, and the panel of hard-nosed journalists appearing with him were no softer.

When he arrived at the studio, Jack told Spivak, "I suppose you're ready to throw me some of your curves."

Spivak replied, "You know, Senator, I have too high a regard for you to pull my punches."

Countered Kennedy, "Never mind that stuff, just lower your regard."

Even though Jackie had to curtail her activities because of her pregnancy — the baby was due before the end of the year — she campaigned as hard as she was able. She was with Jack for the primaries in the snows of New Hampshire and Wisconsin, and in the bleak poverty areas of West Virginia. Later, she gave teas and receptions, wrote a weekly newsletter, and used her knowledge of foreign languages to win over Spanish, Italian, and French voters.

Marveling at her fluency before a Hispanic audience in New York, Jack stepped to the microphone when she concluded and said, "My wife can also speak English."

Although Jackie did not appear often in public during the campaign, she drew enormous crowds when she did. Once Dave Powers turned to the candidate at a rally and told him, "Half the people have come to see Jackie, not you."

In California, Kennedy was asked why Jackie was not with him. "She's home," he answered, "having a boy." Later, newspersons wanted to know how he knew Jackie would have a son.

"She told me," he replied.

Because she had little conception of what went on outside the social and arts worlds, Jackie made gaffes. In Kenosha, Wisconsin, she was sent onto an auditorium stage to warm up the crowd before the appearance of the candidate.

She began haltingly, then decided that community singing would put them all in a good mood. "Let's all sing 'Southie Is My Hometown,' " she announced. The song is virtually the national anthem in South Boston, but Kenoshans had never heard of it. They stared at her in puzzlement and Jackie sang alone.

Jackie could not give up her elegant ways. Once she greeted newspersons in her and Jack's Georgetown home wearing beautifully tailored purple slacks by Emilio Pucci, and lounged like an odalisque on the carpet as she wisecracked her way through the questions. Pat Nixon, Jack knew, was giving *her* interviews wearing off-the-rack dresses all women recognized as inexpensive, and discussed children, husbands, and homemaking. "Good God!" he groaned. "She's cost me thousands of votes!"

Mrs. Kennedy made up for these blunders when she was sent to calm an audience of Polish-Americans in Milwaukee that had become restless because the candidate was late.

After Jack and Jackie finally arrived, Jackie went on first to address the 3,000 persons who had jammed the hall and, by then, were shuffling their feet and even starting to boo.

"We're terribly sorry to have kept you waiting so long when you've been so nice to come," she said in her whispery voice. The hall quieted down as she continued. "With so much to do in a campaign, it's a wonder that more mistakes aren't made which inconvenience people who are so kind and thoughtful as to encourage the candidate."

By then she had most of them in the palm of her hand.

She got the rest with her brief conclusion: "I have great respect and affection for the Polish people," she said. "Besides, my sister is married to a Pole." [Lee had married Prince Stanislas Radziwill.]

Then, in an authentic accent, she ended with: *"Polska bedzie zyla zawsze!"* "Poland will live forever!" She sat down amid roars of approval.

On the platform, Jack turned to Paul B. Fay, Jr., later his Undersecretary of the Navy, and asked, "How would you like to try and follow that?"

During the campaign, much criticism, some of it good-natured, but a lot of it bitter, was directed at Jack, Bobby, and the hard-charging Kennedys for their overarching ambition and the money they were willing to spend to achieve their goals.

Barry Goldwater, personally friendly but politically antagonistic, said, "I sincerely fear for my country if John Kennedy should be elected President. The fellow has absolutely no principles. Money and gall are all the Kennedys have."

Lyndon Johnson alluded to the Kennedy fortune: "I haven't had anything given to me. Whatever I have and whatever I hope to get will be because of whatever energy and talents I have."

Bobby's brash tactics as his brother's campaign director were likened by a British correspondent to those of a "Sioux brave about to take a scalp."

At Gridiron press dinners in Washington, the kidding was gentler. To the tune of "My Heart Belongs to Daddy," this was sung:

> We sent all our bills to Daddy
> 'Cause Daddy pays them so well.

To "All of Me," Joe, Sr., took this ribbing:

> All of us

Why not take all of us?
Fabulous —
You can't live without us.
My son Jack
Heads the procession.
Then comes Bob,
Groomed for succession. . . .

No Catholic had ever been elected President. In 1928 Alfred E. Smith, a governor of New York, had been soundly defeated by F.D.R., and since then no member of the Catholic faith had been nominated by either party. Kennedy's Catholicism, then, was a formidable hurdle to vault on his way to the White House.

As the campaign progressed, opposition to J.F.K. by those who feared he would be influenced by Church doctrine was rising rapidly. The criticism dismayed and angered him. "I'm getting tired of these people who think I want to replace the gold at Fort Knox with a supply of holy water," he told aides.

The attention given the religious issue puzzled Jackie. "I think it's so unjust of people to be against Jack because he's a Catholic," she said. "He's such a poor Catholic."

Kennedy had spoken out many times on the separation of Church and State. During the primary campaign in West Virginia, he had told a television audience he believed deeply in the wall between the two that developed under the Constitution.

"If a President breaks his oath, he is not only committing a crime against the Constitution, for which Congress can impeach and should impeach him, but he is committing a sin against his God," he said.

In 1959, he wrote to a Colorado woman: "It is my firm belief that there should be separation of Church and State as we understand it in the United States — that is, both Church and State should be free to operate, without interference from each other, in their respective areas of jurisdiction."

And in 1957, he told writer Andre Fontaine in *McCall's* magazine: "Nobody in my Church gives me orders. It doesn't work that way. I've been in Congress for ten years and it has never happened. I can't act as a private individual does. My responsibility is to my constituents and to the Constitution. So if it came to a conflict between the two, and not just a personal moral issue, I am bound to act for the interests of the many."

Jokes about Kennedy and his Catholicism abounded:

If Kennedy became President, the Statue of Liberty would be renamed Our Lady of the Harbor.

A law would be passed making it mandatory for all non-Catholics to ride in the rear seats of buses.

Signs were posted in parts of Chicago: "Attend the church of your choice — while there is still time."

"Kennedy quarters" were circulated — the regular twenty-five-cent pieces with George Washington's profile retouched with red to make it resemble that of Pope John.

A nightclub comic said that the Kennedys sent old Joe a birthday card that read: "To our father, who art in Hyannis Port."

Even Jack himself quipped, "Now I understand why Henry the Eighth set up his own church."

His favorite line during the entire controversy came from Pope John XXIII, the seventy-nine-year-old pontiff who was trying to learn English and having a tough time of it. The Pope, of course, had heard all the stories of how America would be ruled by the Vatican if a Catholic were elected President. Asked by a U.S. bishop if he thought Kennedy could win, he replied, "Do not expect me to run a country with a language as difficult as yours."

Former President Truman, irritated by G.O.P. rhetoric during the campaign, exploded one day. "As far as I'm concerned, the Republicans can go to hell!"

Jack immediately sent him the following wire:

> Dear Mr. President, I have noted with interest your suggestion as to where those who vote for my opponent should go. While I understand and sympathize with your deep motivation, I think it is important that our side try to refrain from raising the religious issue.

In Los Angeles, a reporter asked him, "Do you think a Protestant can be elected President in 1960?" The audience at the Los Angeles Press Club laughed at the twist on the question Kennedy was facing.

Kennedy replied, "If he's prepared to answer how he stands on the issue of separation of

Church and State, I see no reason why we should discriminate against him."

Jack knew he would have to face down his critics sooner or later, but hadn't made up his mind when or where, until he received an invitation to address the Houston Ministerial Conference on September 12. He agreed to go.

In the ballroom of the Rice Hotel he made one of the three most important speeches of his life. Another was the inaugural address, in which he made the ringing call: "And so, my fellow Americans, ask not what your country can do for you; ask what you can do for your country." The third was his civil-rights speech in 1963.

Facing the ministers, dozens of newspapers, hundreds of spectators, and a battery of microphones, he enunciated his position clearly:

> I believe in an America where the separation of Church and State is absolute. Where no Catholic prelate should tell the President, should he be Catholic, how to act. And no Protestant minister would tell his parishioners for whom to vote. Where no church or church school is granted any public funds or political preference, and where no man is denied public office merely because his religion differs from the President who might appoint him or the people who might elect him.
>
> I believe in an America that is officially neither Catholic, Protestant, nor Jewish.

135

Where no public official either requests or accepts instructions on public policy from the Pope, the National Council of Churches, or any other ecclesiastical source. Where no religious body seeks to impose its will, directly or indirectly, upon the general populace or the public acts of its officials. And where religious liberty is so indivisible that an act against one church is treated as an act against all.

For while this year it may be a Catholic against whom the finger of suspicion is pointed, in other years it has been, and may someday be again, a Jew, or a Quaker, or a Unitarian, or a Baptist. It was Virginia's harassment of Baptist preachers, for example, that led to Jefferson's statute of religious freedom. Today I may be the victim, but tomorrow it may be you. Until the whole fabric of our harmonious society is ripped apart at a time of great national peril.

Finally, I believe in an America where religious intolerance will someday end, where all men and all churches are treated as equals, where every man has the same right to attend or not to attend the church of his choice; where there is no Catholic vote, no anti-Catholic vote, no bloc voting of any kind, and where Catholics, Protestants, and Jews at both the lay and the pastoral levels will refrain from those attitudes of disdain and division which have so often marred their works in the past, and promote instead the American idea of brotherhood.

This is the kind of America I believe in, and this is the kind of America I fought for in the South Pacific and the kind my brother died for in Europe. But I do not intend to apologize for these views to my critics of either Catholic or Protestant faith. Nor do I intend to disavow either my views or my Church in order to win this election. If I should lose on the real issues, I shall return to my seat in the Senate, satisfied that I tried my best and was fairly judged. But if this election is decided on the basis that forty million Americans lost their chance of being President on the day they were baptized, then it is the whole nation that will be the loser in the eyes of Catholics and non-Catholics around the world, in the eyes of history, and in the eyes of our own people.

Watching on television, Sam Rayburn, who, at best, had been a lukewarm supporter, shouted, "By God, look at him, and listen to him. He's eating them blood-raw!"

The speech was a watershed for Kennedy's candidacy. It helped clear the air of the troublesome religious issue, which, from then on, lost steam.

Knowing that his brother, with his looks, charm, and grace, was perfect for television, Bobby insisted that considerable time and money must be spent on TV commercials and telecast speeches, and that TV stations be given top priority in the coverage of Jack's appearances. It worked.

Said Ted Sorensen, "Without this medium . . . John Kennedy would never have been elected President."

Despite vigorous campaigning, neither Kennedy nor his Republican opponent, Richard M. Nixon, was creating a significant impression on the voters. Kennedy was looked upon in the main as a nice young fellow who wanted to sit in the Oval Office, Nixon as an opportunist, with ideas not much different from Kennedy's, who would do anything to get there. Comedian Mort Sahl summed up the blandness with which both were regarded: "I don't think either of them can win."

Equally acidulous were bumper stickers that cropped up in California: "Be thankful only one of them can win."

The four Kennedy-Nixon debates, televised nationally late in September and in October, changed that view completely. Jack Kennedy shattered the immaturity image that had dogged him and emerged as a strong, aggressive candidate, very sure of himself and the issues for which he stood, able to think quickly on his feet, marshal facts, and put his points across clearly and succinctly. And the voters liked those points: swift action on housing, education, and price stability; regaining the initiative in the cold war then existing with the Soviet Union; infusing youth and dynamism into government.

A debating champion in high school and an expert in swaying large audiences, Nixon was nonetheless unsure how he'd perform against the tough-minded intellectual from Massachusetts. "They expect me to wipe up the floor with this guy," he complained to his advisers.

His apprehensions were well founded. Jack was calm and self-possessed, making his points crisply and cleanly; Nixon seemed to have stage fright as he sweated his way through his answers, his hands noticeably trembling as they held the lectern.

But the finishing blow was his haggard appearance on the television screens of 70,000,000 viewers. He had asked only for a light powder to cover his heavy beard, a disastrous decision. Under the bright lights, the makeup was useless; he looked pale and sickly, instead of appearing as a robust, healthy candidate who sought to lead the nation.

Bobby Kennedy was responsible for the makeup debacle. A high-ranking member of the Nixon staff, aware that Bobby had more experience in television than anyone there, asked him if he thought Nixon's makeup was all right. Bobby knew it wasn't, but gave the okay sign, saying, "Terrific! terrific! I wouldn't change a thing!"

On Election Day, the Big House at Hyannis Port was transformed into the vote-tabulating center for J.F. K. More than a dozen secretaries received the latest tallies from precincts across the nation and relayed them to tabulators set up in the living room, where Lou Harris and his staff of expert pollsters studied them for what they portended.

By three A.M., Jack had won 261 electoral votes, but needed 269 for election. Still not heard from were California, with 32 electoral votes; Illinois, with 27; and Minnesota, with 14. Victory was close, but Nixon was not conceding. Jack drifted into the kitchen with his mother and several aides, ate a sandwich, and, at about four, said he was going to bed. Jackie had turned in before midnight, certain her husband had won. "Oh, Bunny, you're President now!" she had said.

Jack left through the kitchen exit and walked across the yellowing lawn to his own house. Rose looked at his retreating figure and whispered, "Good night, Mr. President."

J.F.K. awoke at nine and eased himself into a hot bath. While there, Ted Sorensen and Pierre Salinger told him that he had lost California but won Illinois, and that Minnesota had put him over the top. At noon, Nixon sent his press aide, Herbert Klein, to the television cameras to concede the election to John Kennedy. He would not go himself, prompting Jack, who despised him, to comment, "He went out the way he came in — no class."

The election was a squeaker. Jack polled 34,227,096 popular votes to Nixon's 34,108,546, winning by only 118,550, though his electoral count was 302 to his opponent's 219.

In the afternoon, he donned a windbreaker and, trailed by the Secret Service, walked on the beach, watching the waves come in from the Sound and contemplating the awesome responsibilities that lay ahead.

Part Two

Inside Camelot

Chapter Six

Young Mr. President

At forty-three, John Kennedy was the youngest man to be elected President of the United States. Weeks before his inauguration he began to work on his administration. There was much to be done in the next seventy-two days — the White House staff had to be selected, a Cabinet chosen, a budget devised, and a legislative program planned.

Shuttling between his father's Palm Beach estate, his own Georgetown home, and a suite at the Hotel Carlyle in New York City, Kennedy began to shape his New Frontier. He appointed Ted Sorensen as special counsel to the President, put Kenneth O'Donnell in charge of administration and appointments, and made Pierre Salinger the press secretary. Brother-in-law Sargent Shriver was chosen to lead the search to fill the 75 key Cabinet and policy posts and 1,200 lower-level jobs. Clark Clifford, a prominent Washington attorney and a special counsel to President Truman, and Columbia

University Professor Richard Neustadt were tapped to help develop the legislative thrust and strategies for the Kennedy Presidency.

Kennedy's appointment of his brother, Bobby, to the post of Attorney General, an act demanded by old Joe Kennedy, was probably the most controversial of his Cabinet choices.

On Thanksgiving Day, J.F.K. joined Jackie in Washington, where she was awaiting the birth of a baby. After dinner, he boarded a plane to fly back to Palm Beach but learned by radio that his wife had been taken to the hospital. He returned to Washington and arrived after his son was born.

At Palm Beach again, Kennedy was visited by Allen Dulles, director of the Central Intelligence Agency, and Richard Bissell, deputy director, who informed him that the C.I.A. had been organizing and training troops for an assault on the Cuban coast. Later, on the day before the inauguration, President Eisenhower again told Kennedy it was the "policy of this government" to aid anti-Castro forces and he recommended that it be continued.

The thermometer registered in the low twenties on January 20, 1961, Inauguration Day. First Kennedy attended mass at the Holy Trinity Roman Catholic Church in Georgetown. Then he and Jackie went to the White House for coffee with President Eisenhower and his wife, Mamie, in the Red Room.

At twelve fifty-one P.M., Kennedy took the oath of office as the nation's thirty-fifth President on the steps of the Capitol, his hand resting on the Fitzgerald family Bible. The ceremony was followed by a four-hour parade and, in the evening, five inaugural balls. The evening before, with Washington traffic at a standstill because of heavy snowfall, the Kennedys had attended an inaugural concert and a gala, arranged by Frank Sinatra.

Family Ties

Following his election, Kennedy told a cheering crowd at the Hyannis Port Armory that he was off to prepare for a new administration "and a new baby." Jackie, eight months pregnant, was at his side.

Two weeks later, after a quick trip to Texas for talks with his Vice-President, Lyndon B. Johnson, Kennedy flew to the family villa in Palm Beach for staff conferences pertaining to the Cabinet.

No sooner had he landed when word was flashed from Washington that Jackie was hemorrhaging and had been rushed to Georgetown University Hospital. The plane carrying the press was fueled and ready for departure, so Kennedy and his closest friends raced aboard and flew back home. At twelve twenty-two A.M., as they flew over Virginia, there came another message: The new baby had arrived, born by emergency Cesarian section. Kennedy now had a healthy son, weighing six pounds and three ounces.

The U.S. Census Bureau announced that the boy's arrival had increased the nation's population to 182,000,267. The Internal Revenue Service also issued a bulletin: John Kennedy now had an additional tax deduction of $600 a year. Yet another fact about the birth of the boy, who would be named John F. Kennedy, Jr.: He was the first child in the country's history to be born to a President-elect and his wife.

At the hospital, John Kennedy couldn't tell whom his infant son resembled. To newspersons who asked, he acted like any other happy but confused father. "I'll have to study him a little more," he confessed.

Jack knew the choice of Bobby as Attorney General would unleash an avalanche of charges of nepotism. Asked how he planned to make the announcement, he said he'd do it in a way least likely to get press attention. He said that on a dark night he would peer out the door to make sure the street was empty. "Then I'll whisper the announcement and quickly close the door," he declared.

The appointment did cause the predictable furor. Said Jack, straight-faced, "I have been criticized for appointing my brother, but I don't see anything wrong about giving him a little experience before he goes out to practice law."

Bobby, who had to be persuaded to take the job, never lost sight of the fact that his appointment was controversial. Addressing a group of young attorneys in the Department of Justice after his confirmation, he told about his rise to Cabinet status.

"I started in the department as a young lawyer in 1950," he said. "The salary was only four thousand dollars a year, but I worked hard. I was ambitious. I studied. I applied myself.

"And then my brother was elected President of the United States."

Bobby was the butt of many wisecracks about his age. Here are two:

A pre-teen girl wearing a muff, pillbox hat, and Jackie-style hairdo entered an elevator. A passenger glanced at her and remarked to a friend that she looked like Jackie. "You're mistaken," the friend replied. "She's a little young. Must be Bobby's wife."

The Boy Scouts announced that eight of the ten new Cabinet members were once Scouts themselves. A reporter cracked, "One of them still is."

Old Joe was nothing if not realistic. He knew his reputation for conservatism could harm his President son if it was thought he would attempt to influence him. And so, having fulfilled the ambition of a lifetime by seeing a son in the White House, he made a deliberate attempt to fade into the background.

In Los Angeles during the Democratic convention, he had arrived in the city secretly and remained hidden in a huge mansion once belonging to Marion Davies, the former movie star. Few knew he was there, but Joe had a battery of telephones installed near the swimming pool so that he could keep in constant touch with Jack's headquarters at the Biltmore Hotel. After the nomination, he slipped out of town as quietly as he arrived.

He never appeared in public with Jack during the entire campaign. Even after the election, he did not want the nation to see him and perhaps get the notion that his policies would in some way affect the new administration.

On the morning after his election, Jack departed the family house and entered a car for the short ride to the Hyannis Port Armory, where he would address the nation. As the motorcade started off, Jack looked around and realized his father was not present. Peering out, he spotted Joe in the shadows at the far end of the big porch.

The new President got out of the car and went to his father. He leaned over him, talking quietly, obviously urging the old man to come along. At first Joe shook his head. Then, as Jack persisted, he rose and entered Jack's car.

At the armory, he stood by as his President son spoke to the country. The hope of a lifetime had been realized for Joe Kennedy.

J.F.K.'s inaugural address, delivered on a freezing day, captured the mood of the nation and set the course for his administration. It was written by Ted Sorensen but edited and altered countless times over many weeks by John Kennedy. Historians rank it as one of the finest ever given by an American President. He said, in part:

> Let the word go forth from this time and place, to friend and foe alike, that the torch has been passed to a new generation of Americans, born in this century, tempered by war, disciplined by a hard and bitter peace, proud of our ancient heritage, and unwilling to witness or permit

the slow undoing of those human rights to which this nation has always been committed, and to which we are committed today at home and around the world. . . .

Let every nation know, whether it wishes us well or ill, that we shall pay any price, bear any burden, meet any hardship, support any friend, oppose any foe to assure the survival and the success of liberty.

This much we pledge — and more.

To those old allies whose culture and spiritual origins we share, we pledge the loyalty of faithful friends. United, there is little we cannot do in a host of cooperative ventures. Divided, there is little we can do, for we dare not meet a powerful challenge at odds and split asunder.

To those new states whom we welcome to the ranks of the free, we pledge our word that one form of colonial control shall not have passed away merely to be replaced by a far more iron tyranny. We shall not always expect to find them supporting our view. But we shall always hope to find them strongly supporting their own freedom, and to remember that, in the past, those who foolishly sought power by riding the back of the tiger ended up inside. . . .

In the long history of the world, only a few generations have been granted the role of defending freedom in its hour of maximum danger. I do not shrink from this responsibility. I welcome it. I do not believe that any of us would exchange places with any other people or any other generation. The energy, the faith, the devotion which we bring to this endeavor will light our country and all who serve it, and the glow from that fire can truly light the world.

And so, my fellow Americans, ask not what your country can do for you, ask what you can do for your country.

My fellow citizens of the world, ask not what America will do for you, but what together we can do for the freedom of man.

Finally, whether you are citizens of America or citizens of the world, ask of us here the same high standards of strength and sacrifice which we ask of you. With a good conscience our only sure reward, with history the final judge of our deeds, let us go forth to lead the land we love, asking His blessing and His help, but knowing that here on earth God's work must truly be our own.

On the most important day of his life, Jack Kennedy, dressed in a dark jacket, striped pants, a tie with small checks, his coat on his arm and top hat in his hand, was waiting for his wife. Jackie, however, was not ready.

She was upstairs in the Georgetown house fussing with her makeup. It took longer to do this than to dress. Downstairs, Jack had finished rehearsing his inaugural address. He glanced nervously at his watch. They were due at eleven A.M.

at the north portico of the White House to be greeted by President Eisenhower and ride with him to the inaugural stand.

Minutes passed and Jackie still had not appeared. Her husband, by now at the explosion point, hollered loud enough to be heard on the next block: "For God's sake, Jackie, it's late! *Let's go!*"

Joe's efforts at anonymity were abruptly punctured at one of the inauguration balls. Grinning happily, he walked into a hotel into the path of the spotlights that played on him as he removed his topcoat. At the same time, however, he accidentally also took off his tailcoat and stood before the throng in shirt-sleeves and suspenders.

Several thousand guests who were watching exploded into laughter. Embarrassed, Joe managed a small grin and waved to the throng.

Said one onlooker, "It was like a scene from a low comedy routine at a burlesque show."

Music conductor Leonard Bernstein made what he called an "inexcusable blunder" at one of the inaugural balls — he cut in on the President of the United States.

"He was dancing with a friend of mine with whom I wished to dance," Bernstein said, "and since people were cutting in all over the floor, I thought nothing of doing likewise, except that I had forgotten that I was cutting in on the President. He did look pale for a moment, but he got over it and it didn't injure our relationship. He was very sweet about it."

And the girl?

"She was furious," Bernstein admitted.

Sunday morning, two days after his inauguration, Kennedy attended mass at the Holy Trinity Church in Georgetown. As he was driven from the White House, he asked the chauffeur to swing past his home on N Street. There he saw, like many persons who go away for extended periods, that the newspapers were still being delivered despite requests that they be halted. The steps and front yard were littered with old copies.

"Stop the car," he ordered.

He emerged and then returned with an armload, which he dumped into his limo, saying, "I can just hear some of my good Republican neighbors delight in spreading the story, 'How can he run the country if he can't organize his own home?' "

Several hours later, back at the Presidential mansion, Jack invited Teddy and Red Fay to see the Oval Office. It was bare, except for a couple of couches and the desk and chair used by his predecessor, General Eisenhower. As Kennedy spun around in the chair, he said, "Paul, what do you think?"

It all seemed unreal to Fay. "I feel any minute now," he answered, "that some guy is going to stick his head through one of those doors and say, 'All right, you three guys — out of here."

Before the inauguration Jackie had gone to the White House for a basement-to-top-floor inspection. To ease the strain of the tour, her doctor had ordered a wheelchair for her. When Jackie arrived at the White House, she looked around. Not seeing the chair, she spent the entire day on her feet. Exhausted, she was ordered to bed for two weeks.

But the chair was there all the time, discreetly tucked away near the elevator. White House servants had been instructed to bring it out as soon as the new First Lady asked for it.

But she didn't. She explained later, "I was too scared of Mrs. Eisenhower."

Jackie wasted no time starting the massive task of redecorating the White House. She began soon after Election Day by engaging Mrs. Henry Parish, a New York decorator, to hunt for new fabrics and carpeting. The inauguration was on Friday, January 20, and by the following Monday the seven-room family quarters on the second floor of the mansion was a hive of activity — painters were painting, carpenters were hammering, electricians were wiring, plumbers were laying pipe, and furniture movers were weaving around them as they carted in new couches, tables, and chairs for the Kennedys.

Jackie was calm amid the shambles, issuing crisp orders. At her side was Sister Parish. During the morning Jackie asked that, at noon, broiled hamburgers with side dishes of vegetables be served on trays placed wherever there was the least commotion.

When lunch was brought in, four butlers suddenly materialized; two stood stiffly behind each woman as they would at a state dinner. Jackie, glancing behind her, giggled at the sight of the four retainers in attendance at a hamburger lunch.

153

The President came up from the Oval Office and had his own lunch, a glass of Metracal, before retiring to his bedroom for a brief nap. On the way back to his office, he saw that the women had not finished the large hamburgers. J.F.K. polished them off, along with some leftover vegetables, then returned to work.

By mid-February the living quarters had been changed from homespun middle-American to upper-class elegant. The Eisenhowers had preferred a simple decor, livable and comfortable, with heavy furniture and drapes. Jackie transformed the rooms into her own image: bright, sophisticated, refined. Most of the walls were painted a soft white on which she hung paintings and drawings; bright new fabrics took the place of the Eisenhower drapes; and the furniture of the Eisenhower administration was carted off and replaced by graceful period pieces.

One of the severely furnished guest chambers was turned into a cheery bedroom for Caroline, dominated by a white-canopied bed and filled with her collection of stuffed animals and a large rocking horse. Another room, painted blue and white, became the nursery for John, Jr.

A small bedroom that had been reserved for Mamie's elderly mother, Elivera Doud, became a kitchen. Ike had had a tiny one installed in the family quarters so he could prepare his famous vegetable soup, but Jackie wanted more elaborate cooking facilities for the preparation of the family's meals.

On their first evening in the White House, dinner had been a disaster. Because the family dining room on the first floor was a long way from the downstairs kitchen, food arrived late and cold, testing J.F.K.'s patience. Jackie had had enough, too: she decided to turn one of the upstairs bedrooms into a small, cozy dining room, close enough to the new kitchen so that meals could be served promptly — and hot.

The Eisenhowers, who had lived on army bases most of their married life, were uncomfortable in a home that exuded grandeur and historical significance. Their White House reflected their tastes, which were middle-class suburbia, simple and homey. Said Jackie, "The place almost sent me back to the hospital with a crying jag."

So she did what every wife would do in a new home — redecorate. The money, $100,000, came from the U.S. Treasury. It was the amount allotted by Congress for the refurbishing of family quarters as well as restoring the house. It was clearly not enough; — private donations and foraging in government warehouses, back rooms of museums, and in the White House itself had to make up the difference.

Artworks, antiques, and valuable pieces of furniture — some 240 in all — were donated outright during the next three years. Jackie's forays into the warehouses and museums uncovered portraits of American Indians, a number of Paul Cézanne paintings, some pieces of a china service purchased by Abraham Lincoln, and valuable rugs ordered by Theodore Roosevelt, among many others.

One of her proudest discoveries was an elaborately carved desk built out of timbers from the

British warship *Resolute* and presented to Rutherford B. Hayes by Great Britain. It was moved to the Oval Office and used by J.F.K. throughout his administration. (It can now be seen at the Kennedy Library, south of Boston.)

One day, while prowling the halls and storerooms of the mansion, Jackie entered a large, and unused, men's room in the basement. In a large closet inside, she found beautiful marble busts of George Washington, Martin Van Buren, Christopher Columbus, and other historical figures. They had been stashed away during a previous administration and were long forgotten.

She ordered them cleaned and placed in prominent positions in the galleries of the mansion, where visitors admired them, never knowing they had once reposed in a men's toilet.

The new First Lady put great effort into making the mansion a "truly historic house." While J.F.K. did not get involved in the actual planning or selection of furnishings, he, of course, had the final say as to what changes were made. When Jackie revamped the Blue Room, Jack was unhappy with the results.

"Before you open it up [to the public]," he said to Chief Usher J. B. West, "have the floors darkened and get a great big blue rug on the floor."

After Jackie taped her tour of the state rooms for CBS-TV in February, 1962, the White House staff — along with President and Mrs. Kennedy — went to the theater downstairs to watch the program.

"It's terrific," marveled J.F.K. "Terrific. Can we show it in 1964?"

It is not unusual for a landlord to refuse to rent premises to a family for any of a number of reasons. But to the First Family. . . ?

Soon after the inauguration, after a long search, the President and Jackie found what they considered an ideal weekend retreat. Called Glen Ora, it was a four-hundred-acre estate in the midst of the rolling Virginia hunt country near Middleburg, to the west of Washington and only about an hour's drive away. It afforded peace, privacy, charm, and plenty of space in which Caroline could romp. They signed a lease.

Much had to be done to get the large stucco house ready for a Presidental tenant. New carpeting was laid, furniture was reupholstered or changed, rooms were painted and papered, and curtains were hung. By late February, the place was ready and the Kennedys came down for their first weekend.

When John Kennedy met his landlord for the first time, he committed a gaffe. Upon his introduction to Gladys Tartiere, who had purchased Glen Ora with her late husband, Raymond, two decades before, he remarked, "Your house cost me a lot of money."

Mrs. Tartiere was astonished and annoyed. A year later, Clark Clifford, J.F.K.'s personal lawyer, told Mrs. Tartiere that the President might want to renew his lease on the property and even purchase it eventually.

But, said Mary Van Rensselaer Thayer, Jackie's lifelong friend, Gladys Tartiere turned him down.

Jackie's three babies, Caroline, John, Jr., and Patrick, were delivered by Cesarian section. Of Ethel

Kennedy's eleven children, the last four were Cesarian births, as were the last two of Eunice Shriver, Jack's sister. When Cesarians were not performed, none of the Kennedy wives used any of the so-called painless or natural-childbirth techniques. Some received a general anesthetic, others a regional one that left them fully conscious but blocked pain from the lower part of the body.

Jackie did not nurse her babies. Along with all the other Kennedy mothers, she used prepared formulas. Ethel was the only one to nurse, but she, too, switched to bottle feeding after the first four of her eleven children.

Jackie had always found it hard to be a "Kennedy woman." After one disastrous experience when she was injured in a touch-football game, she never allowed herself to be drafted onto a team. She knew little and cared less about politics and politicians. But she adopted one of the Kennedy practices when it came to babies.

All Kennedy mothers, says Luella Donovan, the former family nurse, would have long "conversations" with their infants upon their first meetings. She said:

"When the babies were brought to them twelve to twenty-four hours after they were born, they started communicating with them intimately. They talked softly to them, pouring out their feelings, telling them the secrets they'd had in their hearts the last nine months, explaining how much they were wanted, how much they would be loved, how anxious their brothers and sisters were to see them. It was real talk, not just a chucking under the chin or a few words about how beautiful they are.

"What astonished me always was the reaction of the babies. They would look up at the faces of their mothers, as though seeing them and hearing their words. Actually, of course, they did not see at all, but they did hear. The first of our senses to develop is hearing. The soft, soothing tones, I am convinced, seeped into some level of the babies' immature consciousness, and they responded.

"I don't know whether one Kennedy mother passed this little custom on to another, or how it was adopted, but Jackie did it, too. And I always left them alone at this time because they had their little secrets to share with their new babies."

In August, 1963, Jackie again gave birth prematurely, this time to a boy weighing only five pounds. Within a few hours, doctors discovered that the infant was suffering from hyaline membrane disease, or respiratory distress syndrome, which at that time was fatal in about seventy-five percent of the cases. It occurs mostly in preemies whose lungs are insufficiently developed.

The baby, named Patrick Bouvier Kennedy, lived less than two days. Ironically, advances in treatment make it possible today for doctors to save three out of four victims.

Jack was at the hospital the entire time. When doctors told him little Patrick was gone, he went to the end of the hospital corridor and struck the wall futilely with his fists. Then he walked to the boiler room, where Pierre Salinger saw him weeping uncontrollably. He wept again during mass for the infant at the home of Richard Cardinal Cushing in Boston, where he embraced Patrick's tiny coffin.

Gently, Cushing told him, "Jack, you'd better get along. Death isn't the end of all, but the beginning."

After the burial in a cemetery in Brookline, the President didn't want to leave. He knelt and put his hand on the newly spaded earth and was heard to whisper, "It's awful lonely here."

After little Patrick died, Aristotle Onassis told Jackie's sister, Lee, that his yacht, the *Christina*, was at the First Lady's disposal for her recuperation. She could sail wherever she wanted, for as long as she wanted, on his floating palace. And a palace it was. Winston Churchill, a frequent guest, had called it "the most magnificent yacht in the world."

The all-white vessel with yellow funnel was 60 feet longer than a football field, weighed 2,200 tons, and had a swimming pool, a sickbay superior to many small hospitals, and guest suites furnished with antiques, Persian carpets. and satin drapes. The ship's bar, a large circular room, had stools covered with skin from whales' testicles. On the walls of the dining room were original oils by the French painter Marcel Vertes, whose work is exhibited in the Louvre; on the tables were exquisite dishes prepared by a master chef.

Jackie accepted Onassis's invitation, and before long Jack Kennedy, back at home, began hearing reports of the incredibly luxurious cruise. There was dancing every night and a 60-man crew to fulfill Jackie's every wish, plus a Swedish masseur and two hairdressers. Newspapers began head-lining Jackie's sybaritic vacation. Representative Oliver Bolton of Ohio, a Republican, pointed out on the House floor that one of the guests aboard the *Christina* was Undersecretary of Commerce Franklin D. Roosevelt, Jr. Mr. Roosevelt's influ-ence with the U.S. Maritime Administration, Bolt-on asserted, could have important consequences for Onassis's shipping interests.

In addition to all of this, Onassis had been in-dicted in 1954 on fraud charges in connection with the purchase of Liberty ships, and, moreover, his association with opera singer Maria Callas and other glamorous women was top-drawer gossip in the U.S. and European capitals.

Jack became increasingly angry as the days went by. Finally he called Jackie from Washington by radio telephone and told her, "I know you're on the high seas, and I don't care how you get off that yacht, but get off!"

When she asked, logically enough, how he ex-pected her to leave the ship while it was cruising in the Aegean Sea, he was said to have retorted, "Jackie, you're a good swimmer!"

Jackie did not dive off the *Christina*, nor did she ask Onassis, who was on board, to dock at the nearest port. She stayed on until the end of the cruise. On the final evening, Onassis gave a din-ner party for Jackie and the other guests and pre-sented her with a diamond-and-ruby necklace. Lee and the other women also received end-of-cruise gifts, an Onassis custom, but none was so magnificent or costly as Jackie's.

Jack, accompanied by Caroline and John, Jr., gave her a warm greeting when she returned to Washington. At the airport there were smiles all around. Nobody knows what happened behind closed doors in the White House that evening.

J.F.K. was irritated by Jackie's association with some of her artistic friends who were obviously effeminate. On one occasion, when she returned from a party at which she was photographed with one, he said in exasperation, "For God's sake, Jackie, can't you steer clear of the Nellie boys until I'm reelected?"

Rose and Jackie rubbed each other the wrong way. Rose felt the First Lady was too regal and aloof, and Jackie resented her mother-in-law for dispensing advice too freely to Jack and everyone else. As a result, Rose seldom visited the mansion while Jackie was there, timing her appearances to coincide with Jackie's absences.

Rose insisted on occupying the Lincoln bedroom when she did visit. The President was showing some distinguished visitors around the upstairs living room once and he flung open the door of the Lincoln Room, then closed it abruptly. His mother was napping on the bed.

Like many persons born in the last century, Rose found it hard to adapt to changing times. She never got over her prudishness, ingrained in her by her straitlaced Boston upbringing and her European convent-school education. Today's looser

moral standards, which permit the use of four-letter words in the movies and on the stage, appall
her.

When movies were shown at the family's private theater at the Hyannis Port compound, they
were always previewed by aides to make sure
they contained no nudity, sex scenes or
vulgar language.

Once she spotted Maria Shriver, the beautiful
brunette daughter of Eunice and Sargent Shriver,
on the compound's lawn dressed in shorts and a
halter top. Rose immediately called Eunice and
told her Maria "should not be running around
with her breasts showing."

In 1962, Jack asked his mother to represent him at
a reception in honor of Scott Carpenter at the Wal-
dorf-Astoria Hotel in Manhattan. Carpenter, one
of the original Project Mercury astronauts, had
just completed his epochal orbit of the earth in the
Aurora 7. He was the second American to accomplish the feat; the first was John H. Glenn, Jr. A
press photographer corralled Rose, Carpenter,
and former Presidents Herbert Hoover and Harry
Truman for a rare picture.

When Rose saw it in the newspaper, she hit the
ceiling. "I had my mouth open," she complained,
"as though I was overwhelmed at greeting both
Presidents." Shortly afterward, she met Truman
again at another reception. He, too, had seen the
offending photograph.

"Mrs. Kennedy," he told her, "if they had taken
a picture like that of my wife, I would have gone
over and punched that photographer in the nose!"

During the Camelot years and for a long time afterward, John, Jr., was called "John-John" by the media because everyone thought, that was what his father called him. He never did.

Dave Powers explains how the name originated: "Once John Kennedy called to his son by name, clapping his hands as he did so. When the boy didn't respond, he clapped his hands again, and again called out John's name. He was overheard, and the 'John-John' name stuck, but the President always called him just John.

"After the double name got going, I asked the President, what would the boy have been called by the media if you'd clapped your hands three times — 'John-John-John?'"

Even at three years of age, John, Jr., was working crowds. Occasionally his nurse, Maude Shaw, took him on shopping trips to Georgetown, where they always drew large knots of people who recognized him at once. They didn't faze him. He would walk up to the nearest person, stick out a small hand, and announce, "My name is John Fitzgerald Kennedy, Junior. What's your name?"

Among his toys in the White House was a small model of the Gemini space capsule in which astronauts were to fly 10 manned missions, proving humans could live and work in space. John soon learned to take the capsule apart and put it back together. When Dave Powers tried to reassemble the capsule, he was stumped by the nose cone, which he couldn't get to fit properly. John took it from him and replaced it with ease.

Jackie could be unkind at times. When the family moved into the White House, a room was needed for Maude Shaw, the children's nurse. A sizable dressing room between Caroline's and John's room was converted into a bedroom for her.

Said Jackie to J. B. West, the chief usher: "She wouldn't need much. Just find a wicker basket for her banana peels and a little table for her false teeth at night."

The buck always stopped at the Oval Office — well, almost always. On at least one occasion the President tried to shift the blame for an order Jackie gave to the White House staff. Jackie wanted each of them to sign a pledge not to reveal anything about the persons and events inside the mansion. Under her instructions, West asked employees to agree.

When the pledge, which was not legally binding, became known, Kennedy was subjected to sharp criticism, and was charged with initiating censorship. He visited West in the latter's office and asked him to take responsibility. When the chief usher admitted he had asked the staff to sign the pledge, Kennedy was relieved.

"Good," he said. "We'll put out a statement saying it was your idea, and you initiated it. It will look more official and less of a personal thing coming from you."

In the Kennedy administration, Secret Service men had to get accustomed to matters that were not part of their rigorous training for the job. On October 14, 1962, the President visited Buffalo,

165

New York, for a Pulaski Day parade. As 200,000 people watched, a six-year-old girl handed him a doll, authentically garbed as a Polish peasant child. "Mr. President," the little girl said, "this is for your little girl, Caroline."

J.F.K. accepted it graciously and placed it next to him on the speaker's platform, where it remained during the ceremonies. Afterward, onlookers were surprised, and delighted, to see the doll cradled in the arm of a burly agent, who carried it throughout the entire day.

Children's parties were not uncommon at the White House, and J.F.K. would put in an appearance whenever he could.

"What does your father do?" he asked one small boy at one of these parties.

"He's in *your* Cabinet," replied the son of Postmaster General Edward Day.

During a news conference at Palm Beach before the inauguration, Caroline had clomped in wearing Mrs. Kennedy's high-heeled shoes. As J.F.K. reached for her to begin to scold her, he heard the press corps roaring with laughter. And then he realized that his actions would be caught on film for the nation to see.

So, with a big smile — masking who knew what — Kennedy led his daughter calmly to the door, unscolded for the moment, at least.

Halloween fell on a Thursday in 1963, a few weeks before the President left for Dallas. In the afternoon, Caroline and John, Jr., dressed as goblins, burst into the Oval Office and danced menacingly around the desk, uttering scary sounds in high, piping voices. Jack, Dave Powers, and Kenny O'Donnell halted their conference and pleaded with the children to spare them. Satisfied that they had terrified the grown-ups, Caroline and John removed their masks.

The first nursery school in the White House evolved from a play group Caroline had attended in Georgetown when her father was a senator. When he became President, Jackie invited the group to meet in the White House, where they were installed in a third-floor solarium, and in good weather, they played outside on the lawn.

Mostly shielded from publicity, the school made a good newspaper story one day. The children were watching from the solarium balcony as the premier of Algeria, Ahmel Ben Bella, arrived by helicopter on the White House grounds. As the customary nineteen-gun salute got under way, one little boy got all charged up.

"Boom-boom!" he cried out each time the guns went off, his words clearly audible to the guests below. Many broke into smiles but the teacher, unaware that the boy could be heard, made no attempt to quiet her charge.

The Little White School House cost parents of its twenty-four students $550 a year each for the salaries of the two teachers and the cost of materials and equipment. Classes were held in two rooms on the third floor, and a playground with swings, slides, and a jungle gym was set up in the President's Park at the rear of the mansion. Often,

J.F.K. would step from his office to watch the kids at play.

Caroline, self-possessed at five, was rebuked by a Secret Service agent one day for being rambunctious. She stopped racing around, looked up at him, and said, "My, we're grumpy today, aren't we?"

She was also competitive, Kennedy style. When her father asked her how she was doing at school, she replied, "I'm the smartest in the class."

The touching photo of three-year-old John, Jr., saluting as the casket bearing his slain father was borne down the steps of St. Matthew's Cathedral on its final journey still brings lumps to throats. John had learned how to salute in the White House.

He loved to play soldier. After hours Dave Powers would take a sword from the Oval Office and march through the corridors, followed by his one-boy regiment. John also watched parades and observed the way soldiers saluted. He would stand stiffly in imitation, hand to forehead. At first he used his left hand, then shifted to the right.

That was why he needed only a whispered suggestion from his mother to salute his dad.

One Sunday Caroline wandered downstairs from the living quarters into the press lobby in the west wing. Startled reporters leaped from the worn leather armchairs and sofas and clustered about her. One asked what her father was doing.

She offered a straight answer, unhedged with political obfuscation: "He's not doing anything.

He's just sitting up there with his shoes and socks off, doing nothing."

The disarming description of Presidential inactivity was flashed out over the wires and appeared in every newspaper and on every television and radio news program. Kennedy grimaced and issued a decree: Caroline would have no more press conferences.

Complained the *Washington Star*: "To muzzle her, a member of such an outspoken family, and in a country so proud of its freedom of speech, would be a grievous error of policy."

Caroline soon discovered the telephone and placed long-distance calls to her friends in Florida, chatting for lengthy periods. For the White House operators, who could track down virtually anybody anywhere for the President, it was no problem to connect Caroline with anyone she wished. When J.F.K. discovered what his daughter was doing, he cracked down — no more long-distance calls were to be put through for her.

Caroline could write her name when she was three, and at four years of age she could add and subtract and memorize long poems her father taught her. Her precocity impressed old Joe, who told Jack, "Your daughter is smarter than you were at her age."

Jack, swelling with pride, retorted, "She sure is. It's heredity. Look at who she has for a father."

The President made up stories to tell Caroline, which often revolved around Caroline's Welsh terrier, Charlie, and her imaginary pet bear, named Bruin. And he often would play the roles of the characters in the stories.

One story the President told Caroline went like this:

"I heard Bruin and Charlie having a chat the other day. Bruin was saying that Charlie must have a soft time living in the White House and Glen Ora, and Charlie was quite angry with Bruin. He said, 'You don't know what you're talking about. I've got a real tough job here. I've acres of ground to patrol. I've got to keep the ducks and the squirrels at the White House in line. I've got to guard Caroline.'"

Many fathers, intrigued by gifts given to their children, spend hours playing with them, while the kids drift off elsewhere. The President of the United States was no exception.

In 1963, when Kennedy visited Europe, President Antonio Segni of Italy gave him a three-foot-long model schooner, perfect in every detail down to the blue-and-red mainsail and the green-and-yellow jib. "For your son, John," Segni explained.

Back at the Cape, John, then two years old, was not very interested. But the President was. With Caroline and Lem Billings, he launched the black-hulled craft into Nantucket Sound and watched it sail off. A strong wind carried it about 100 yards out and then back onto the beach. Caroline and a few of her cousins raced to retrieve it, with Kennedy and Lem following. The two seamen waded into the water and sent the schooner again on its way. They played with it for two hours.

Money Matters

When Jack was elected, his father's wealth was estimated at between $200,000,000 and $400,000,000 in pre-inflation dollars. Thanks to trust funds set up in his name, Jack himself was worth $1,000,000 before he entered his teens and about $10,000,000 when he took office.

Both J.F.K. and Bobby were cavalier about personal finances, stuffing bills into their pockets when they went out, or forgetting to take any cash at all. Both brothers often had to ask aides to buy them candy bars, put money in the collection plate in church, and pay taxi fares.

Charles Spalding said that Jack was "awkward and naïve" about his personal business affairs, and so was Bobby. "Listening to them talk about money was like listening to nuns talk about sex," Spalding declares. "It was something they were totally ill at ease with."

While attending Harvard, Jack agreed to split phone bills equally with his roommates. In 1937, when his father was the U.S. ambassador to Great Britain, young Kennedy talked to his parents, his brothers, and sisters almost every other day, running up immense transatlantic toll charges. Most of the time, his roommates' calls would be either local or to cities fairly close to Cambridge. Once in a while Jack would kick in with his (enormous) share, but most of the time he'd plead, "Gosh, I haven't any cash. You guys take care of it, and I'll pay you back." They did; he didn't.

Unlike Jack, Ted, who came to Harvard in 1950, was rarely without money, but he did not spread it around freely. His former classmates still talk about the time he invited nine friends and their dates to an expensive French restaurant in New York following the Harvard-Princeton football game. They all assumed the dinner would be on Kennedy, but when they filed out of the restaurant after a sumptuous repast, Ted was at the door, pen and paper in hand, collecting each man's share. He kept accurate count, too, charging one fellow an extra seventy-five cents for a second drink he had ordered.

Patsy Mulkern, the colorful Boston pol who campaigned with J.F.K. in his earliest races, once drove him to Logaan Airport to catch a Washington-bound plane. Patsy's girl, Alice, who worked in a drugstore, had given him an envelope containing $34 to pay some bills. At the terminal, Jack—broke as usual—asked Patsy to buy him some candy, *Time* and *Look* magazines, then boarded the plane. In a moment, he reappeared.

"Pat," he said, "have you got any money?"

"Like a fool," Pats·· recalled, "I pulled out that envelope. He grabbed it and ran up the gangplank. 'I'll see you later,' he said. I said, 'Hey, that's Alice's pay you're holding, her money!' And he says, 'See you later.' "

It took a long time, but Patsy finally got Alice's money back. "I thought I'd have to go to court!" he said.

J.F.K. balked at having to spend money. George Smathers recalled that in restaurants Kennedy would run his eyes down the right side of the menu and grouse about the prices. Joe Kennedy, noting the shabbiness of his son's wardrobe when the war ended, sent him and Smathers to a fine store to get some "decent" things to wear. Joe said he'd pick up the tab. Smathers chose pricey garments, while Jack, who checked the price tags before even looking at the clothes, bought the least expensive outfit he could find.

As with other married folks, money quarrels topped the list of disputes between the First Couple. Once, fuming about the bills from couturiers, specialty shops, and department stores, which approached $150,000 in a single year, Jack said, "She's unbelievable. She thinks she can go on spending forever. I don't understand what the hell she's doing with all these things. God, she's driving me crazy, absolutely crazy."

But Jackie wouldn't curtail her shopping sprees and the bills kept coming in. Looking over them one month, Kennedy turned to an aide and asked ruefully, "Is there a Spender's Anonymous?"

Women's Wear Daily, the fashion newspaper, published an article claiming that Jackie spent $30,000 a year on her wardrobe. She wisecracked, "I couldn't spend that much," she said, "unless I wore sable underwear."

Jackie found that her already large clothes closets were too small for her steadily enlarging wardrobe, so she she summoned carpenters to provide additional space. The President walked in while the construction was under way and his face darkened.

"At this rate," he told his wife as he left, "you're going to need the Pentagon for your wardrobe!"

Jackie's response was unrecorded, but the White House mess buzzed with the story for days.

The high cost of running the White House was a constant source of irritation. President Lyndon Johnson went around turning off the lights to cut down on electric bills, but Kennedy saved a lot more by issuing an order that waiters at receptions in the mansion must not open a new champagne or wine bottle until the one previously uncorked was empty.

Reason: After one large social event, he toured the elegant East Room, the largest of the reception areas, and found a large number of bottles a quarter to a half filled with costly Dom Perignon champagne.

Although President Kennedy never ceased to grouse about expenses, he did not use a cent of his salary for himself or his family. He earned $100,000 a year and gave it all to charity.

Chapter Seven

A Very Lively Sex Life

The reputations of the Kennedy men as women chasers is secure. Columnist Max Lerner once wrote that they expressed a "lusty vigor that is very much of the present era."

Author Norman Mailer predicted that J.F.K.'s "thousand days" might be equally famous for its nights, and judging from the avalanche of accounts of the former President's amours, Mailer was probably correct. J.F.K. told an astounded Harold Macmillan, the British prime minister, that unless he had frequent sexual outlets he suffered excruciating headaches. Considering all the stories, one can assume Kennedy did not have many headaches, at least from that cause.

Loaded with money and charm, with a dazzling smile and Irish wit and blarney, he had no trouble attracting women. He had relationships that lasted a few afternoon hours, overnight, several days, and one that went on for several years. A newsman who knew him from boyhood said, "Jack was always ready for a joke, gossip, or a fuck."

Psycho-historians have speculated that the Kennedy males were only following their father's lead in their womanizing, much the same as they heeded his must-win teaching. Nobody knows what, if anything, Joe told his sons about sex, but his promiscuity was there for them to observe firsthand. And there is little doubt that Jack, early on, became imbued with his father's ma-chismo attitude, which called for the sexual conquest and domination of women. Joe showed by his example that it was manly to possess women, and John Kennedy spent his life being manly.

Kennedy wives have faced difficult choices. Unless they looked the other way, their marriages might not have survived. This was true not only of Joe's boys* but the family's forebears as well.

---

*Except for Bobby's reputed affair with Marilyn Monroe, he was not linked to any woman but Ethel. Their marriage has been called one of Washington's most enduring love matches.

Kenny O'Donnell told the author, "I knew this man as well as anybody. I was intimately associated with him for years and knew everything he ever did, and I know for a fact that this Marilyn Monroe story is absolute horseshit." Harris Wofford quotes the President as having said, "Bobby is no fun at night. He's almost like Eleanor Roosevelt."

"Jack the Zipper"

Honey Fitz had his moments. An incident involving Fitzgerald when he was mayor of Boston, and a blond girl named Toodles Ryan, who hawked cigarettes at a local restaurant, is now a forgotten footnote in the city's turbulent political history. In 1914, Honey Fitz was completing a four-year term and, despite a previous announcement that he would leave office, decided to run for reelection. His arch rival through the years, the formidable James M. Curley, who had counted on Fitz's promise to leave, was infuriated.

Challenging Fitzgerald for the Democratic nomination, he announced that he would deliver a series of speeches in which he would compare Mayor Fitzgerald with other eras and leaders throughout history.

True to his word, he gave the first of the addresses, which he called, "Graft, Ancient and Modern." Honey Fitz stood fast. But when the time drew near for the second and third talks — "Libertines from Henry VIII to the Present Day" and "Great Lovers: From Cleopatra to Toodles" —

he buckled. Rather than risk having Curley discuss the young woman, he threw in the towel and quit the race.

Did Rose know about the sexual promiscuity of the Kennedy men, including her husband? She gave no sign, yet she would have had to have been quite naïve *not* to know, and Rose Kennedy was never a naïve woman.

She held her head high through the years. The only statement she ever made about her husband's affair with Gloria Swanson, the sex queen of silent movies, was a denial it ever existed. Her remark came during a discussion the author had with her about the snowstorm of gossip that always surrounded the family.

"You know," she said, "they talked about Mr. Kennedy and me in the early years of our marriage. But I paid no attention to it. Neither did Joe. We were always in love long before we were married and forever after." When Gloria Swanson wrote a book exposing the details of her relationship with Joe, Rose still had nothing to say.

"Of course she knew," wrote Garry Wills, Northwestern University professor of American culture and public policy. "And of course she had to pretend she did not. That kind of acting came naturally to women of her generation and faith and social position."

Rose also knew about her sons' roving eyes for pretty girls. Each time Ted's name was linked to another young charmer — and there were many — Rose managed to find out and made a mental note of the girl's name.

One day in 1980, after Ted's wife, Joan, left their home in McLean, Virginia, to live alone in Boston, the author talked with Rose about the couple. Asked if she could confirm strong rumors then circulating that the marriage was breaking up, she replied frankly that she did not know.

"Then why," the author persisted, "has Joan gone to live up in Boston, while Ted remains in their big home in Virginia?"

A hilarious misunderstanding followed. Rose, then nearing ninety, had a degree of hearing impairment and did not catch the words correctly.

"Virginia?" she demanded. "Who's Virginia? I never heard of *that* one!"

When she was told that Virginia was not a young woman, Rose relaxed.

Over the years, stories about Jack Kennedy's trysts have multiplied like mushrooms after a spring rain. Many, if not most, are untrue. As one former Presidental assistant put it, "No human could possibly have laid all the dames people said he did. He never would have had time to be President, not to mention the energy. Many women who had received a little attention from him have embroidered the story. If they got a smile, it was enlarged to an invitation. If he engaged them in a brief conversation, it was upgraded to a pass. If he flirted with them — it was translated into anything they wanted it to be."

The assistant recalled that one young woman claimed J.F.K. asked her to come to his office during his Senate years to go over a report. Once inside, she said, he practically threw her on a couch and leaped on top of her. "Good Lord!" he said. "The man was suffering the most excruciating pain from recent back surgery. He was on crutches most of the time. He could no more jump on anyone at that time than he could leap to the moon!"

"Even if you discounted ninety percent of what has been alleged," says Harris Wofford, Kennedy's special assistant for civil rights, "the ten percent that is left would add up to a very lively sex life."

He was partial to airline stewardesses before his election to the Presidency, movie stars after. Before his inauguration, he stayed for a short period at the Hotel Carlyle in New York City.

A young reporter for *The New York Times* was assigned to check on which high-ranking persons were coming to see him. After sitting in the hotel for hours, the reporter told his editor, "There's no story. Nobody's going up there but a lot of glamour stars from Hollywood."

Those were the days before the extramarital liaisons of Presidential candidates (and Presidents) made news.

The "lively sex life" generated a bumper crop of jokes. Sample: On an out of-Washington trip, J.F.K. asked a girl to visit him in his hotel suite. She was greeted in the lobby by a Secret Service man who rode up the elevator with her. As they ascended, he began stroking her breasts, thighs, and more private areas.

The girl, first surprised, then angry, demanded, "What do you think you're doing!"

"Sorry," the agent answered. "The President has a busy schedule this afternoon. He hasn't got time for foreplay."

Sexual antics by Presidents or Presidential candidates is not uncommon. It's been a sport engaged in by eminent men from George Washington, who is supposed to have been enamoured of one Sally Fairfax, to Gary Hart, who temporarily dropped out of the race for the Democratic nomination in 1987 when reports of his extramarital relationship with Donna Rice made headlines.

Rumors about Thomas Jefferson and Sally Hemings, a slave, have been argued for almost two hundred years. Grover Cleveland admitted he was the father of an illegitimate child; Warren Harding made love to Nan Britton in a closet in the White House; and Franklin Delano Roosevelt had a long relationship with Lucy Mercer Rutherford.

During World War II news of a purported romance between General Eisenhower and Kay Summersby, a young Irish woman who served as his driver, surfaced both in the United States and Europe. Years later former President Harry S. Truman told of a letter from Eisenhower to Chief of Staff George C. Marshall, asking to be relieved from duty so he could divorce Mamie and marry Kay. Subsequent research turned up no such document.

In 1987, it was reported by journalist Steve Neal in his biography of Wendell Willkie that the Republican candidate opposing F.D.R. in his third-term bid was openly living with Irita Van Doren, book editor of the *New York Herald Tribune*. Their relationship was known to friends, colleagues, and business associates. But, unlike the Hart experience, no newspaperman wrote about it.

Richard M. Nixon was never linked to a woman other than his wife, Pat. Prior to his resignation in 1975, rumors of an affair with a woman in the Far East were whispered in Washington. Members of the press were startled and amused when they learned of this. One highly incredulous correspondent grinned and shouted, "*Halevai!*," a Yiddish word meaning "I wish it were so!"

"That would have been the best thing that ever happened," he explained. "It would have humanized the guy."

Notes on sex in official Washington: Amorous dalliances occur any time of the night — or day — inside as well as outside Government buildings.

Item: When a roll-call vote is about to be taken, buzzers sound in the suites of the senators to summon them to the chamber. Once a distinguished member's private office remained closed after the buzzer went off. An aide, knowing the politician was inside, waited a few minutes, then knocked on the door. When he got no response, he opened it, then immediately shut it again. The lawmaker was on the couch atop a newly hired secretary, oblivious to buzzers.

Item: "Thigh-watching is one of the most popular diversions of the House," said former Representative Donald W. Riegle, Republican of Massachusetts. With miniskirts again fashionable, women who watch congressional sessions from gallery seats should take heed.

Here's how it works: When a pretty girl is spotted in the gallery, and is so intent on the proceedings that she allows one or both thighs to be exposed, word gets around. House members then cast their eyes upward and ogle. Some even move to a better vantage point, going over to "confer" with a colleague and, while in conference, managing to stare upward.

Item: Libidinous senators make passes all the time. When Sally Quinn of the *Washington Post* accepted a senator's invitation for a ride home from a party, she did not expect him to put his hand on her head and pull her close. She drew away, saying, "I thought you were offering me a ride home."

"What do you think, I'm running a taxi service?" he replied.

Final item: John F. Kennedy used the White House to entertain girl friends when Jackie was away. He had nude swimming parties with mixed company downstairs, and one-on-one sessions upstairs. Once Jackie left for their vacation home in Atoka but, unfortunately for Jack, returned because she had left something in the house.

By that time, Jack's pool party was in full swing. Traphes Bryant, the White House kennel keeper, in a surprisingly detailed book, wrote: "Suddenly the ushers were sounding the alarm, and first thing I knew naked bodies were scurrying every which way."

Another time, Bryant was in a corridor when the elevator door opened. "A naked blond office girl ran through the hall between the second-floor kitchen and the door leading to the west hall. Her breasts were swinging as she ran by. There was nothing to do but get out fast and push the basement buttons."

Elizabeth Barrett Browning wrote: *"How much do I love thee/Let me count the ways."*

More than a century later, John F. Kennedy counted *his* ways. According to Bryant, Jack told a friend, "I'm not through with a girl until I've had her three ways."

Few things tested a woman's aplomb more than to discover evidence of her husband's transgression. One day, Bryant said, Jackie found some filmy underwear, not her own, beneath a pillow in Jack's room. Holding it between thumb and forefinger, she went to him and said, with no trace of tremor in her voice, "Would you please shop around and see who these belong to? They're not my size."

The John F. Kennedy-Marilyn Monroe involvement has been explored almost as fully as his handling of the Cuban missile crisis, and needs no further elaboration. It was perhaps inevitable that the star-struck, oversexed young President would ultimately meet the world's reigning sex symbol. His first glimpse of her, in person, elicited an appreciative comment, which might not go down in history alongside Patrick Henry's ". . . I have but one life" or Stephen Decatur's "our country, right or wrong," but it came from the heart (or rather libido) and is herewith recorded.

In May, 1962, Marilyn, sheathed in a flesh-colored gown so tight it seemed to have been sprayed on, sang "Happy Birthday" to Jack at Madison Square Garden in New York City before 15,000 people in the audience, plus many millions watching on television.

Watching, too, a few yards away, was the forty-five-year-old President, who turned to a companion as Marilyn shed her white mink at the lectern on the stage.

The Presidential comment: "What an ass!"

L.B.J., something of a ladies' man himself, was fascinated by tales of his chief's sexual escapades. Bobby Baker, one of his assistants, went to the White House one day for talks on pending legislation. On his return to his office, Baker found three messages waiting: Johnson wanted to see him at once. He rushed to the Senate chamber, where Johnson, as President of the Senate, was presiding.

Baker was summoned to the podium as soon as he entered the room. The business of the Senate stopped as the two conferred; senators, visitors in the gallery, and newspaper people watched the two intently. The Vice-President, his head close to Baker's, was asking: "Is ol' Jack getting much pussy?"

The J.F.K.-Judith Campbell Exner connection has also been widely publicized. It is noteworthy, not for lurid details of his extramarital sex life, which was already fully documented, but because he was once again treading on very thin ice as he did years ago with Inga-Binga Arvad.

Exner was introduced to Kennedy in Las Vegas by Frank Sinatra nine months before Election Day and subsequently hopped between two beds:

Jack's and Salvatore (Sam) Giancana's. To be in the President's bed wasn't all that risky — in those pre-character-issue days, he would face only Jackie's wrath if she found out. Giancana was another matter. He was a Mafia chieftain, who had succeeded to Al Capone's throne as crime king of Chicago. There would be hell to pay if the nation learned its President was sharing a girl friend with the hoodlum his brother Bobby, as Attorney General, was trying to put behind bars.

When the Exner story came out, J.F.K.'s staff rallied 'round their leader. Dave Powers said the only Campbell with which he was familiar was Campbell's Chunky Vegetable Soup. Exner said she had telephoned the White House seventy times, but Ken O'Donnell replied that anyone could call, but getting through to the President was another matter, and Exner never got through.

Of course, these loyal aides were understandably protective of their boss, but J. Edgar Hoover, who had dug tenaciously into Kennedy's personal life, had the facts. He knew all about Judith and her affair with Jack, and knew about her and her Mafia lover. On March 22, 1962, he lunched with the President at the White House and told him that further association with a girl friend of a Mafia boss was not a very good idea.

Jack saw the light. That very day he severed his association with the lush brunette.

Both Monroe and Exner commented on their sexual performances with Jack Kennedy.

Said Judith, "I understood about the position he had to assume in lovemaking when his back was troubling him, but slowly he began excluding all other positions, until finally our lovemaking was reduced to this one position. . . . He wanted the woman to make love to him. I had sensed it for a long time."

Marilyn's observation was briefer: "I made his back feel better."

Host and Hostess

When it came to entertaining guests, the Kennedys broke with tradition by downgrading the customary white-tie-and-tails affairs to the less-formal black tie. The first time invitations went out calling for black tie at a congressional reception, the First Couple got a sound scolding from Washington's unofficial social arbiter, Carolyn Hagner Shaw.

She expressed stern disapproval in the *Washington Star,* deploring the "dropping of our dignified official customs" and reminding ladies that "floor-length gowns, above-elbow gloves, jewels, and lovely hairdos were always worn" at the White House. Mrs. Shaw, daughter of the founder of Washington's Social List, said she was also appalled that the President and First Lady mingled with the guests rather than greeting them stiffly in a receiving line.

Mrs. Shaw's complaints were pocket-vetoed. Except for state dinners for the highest-ranking foreign dignitaries, black tie and informality were in during the Kennedy years, and stuffiness was out.

Even at the more formal dinners, however, the Kennedys sought to create an atmosphere that would put their guests at ease. A corps of deputy hosts, young military aides, was responsible for ensuring that each guest had a good time in the President's house.

The officers, all bachelors in full uniform, met each arrival and explained the protocol of the evening — where to go to be greeted by the President and First Lady; where guests would be seated during dinner, and who would be on either side. Finally the aide would lead the guests to the ballroom, the lady on his arm, to be introduced to the others in attendance.

The Kennedys also entertained friends at what came to be called White House "fun parties," elegant Jackie-style dinners with guests seated at small round tables for which she personally arranged the place cards. The dinners, at which protocol was kept to an absolute minimum, were invariably followed by dancing, often to the music of Lester Lanin, a Kennedy favorite who introduced the twist at the White House.

Jackie's fondness for *haute cuisine* could be seen in the menus selected for state dinners, as well as informal luncheons for special guests at the White House.

When Princess Grace and Prince Rainier of Monaco were luncheon guests in May, 1961, they were served shelled crab *amandine*, spring lamb *à la brochette aux primeurs*, salade mimosa, strawberries Romanoff, and *petits four secs*. For a dinner honoring Prime Minister Jawaharlal Nehru of India a few months later, the chef served up *vol-au-*

189

Lester David and Irene David

vent Maryland, *gigot d'agneau aux flageolets, tomates grillés, epinard à la crème, mousse aux concombres,* and *bombe glacée.* All washed down with fine wines and Dom Perignon, of course.

When they entertained at the White House, the Kennedys were eager to make their guests feel at home. One guest remarked, "Of course it is an event to attend a White House party. But it's such a gay, informal, relaxed evening that you could easily feel you were at a party in Georgetown. You're mindful of the fact that it's the President's house when you enter, but not again until after you've left."

Music conductor Leonard Bernstein compared Eisenhower parties with the ones given by the Kennedys.

Eisenhower dinners: "You couldn't smoke at the dinner table, you couldn't smoke before dinner, and you couldn't smoke after dinner. I am an inveterate smoker, and I had to perform afterward, and I got more and more nervous. There were no drinks served before dinner either. The guest line formed by protocol, not by alphabet. Everything was different then; it was very stiff and not even very pleasant. Dinner was at a huge horseshoe-shaped table at which seventy-five or so people were seated so that nobody could ever really talk to anybody. . . . The food was ordinary, and the wines were inferior. . . ."

Kennedy dinners: "Compare that [the above] to the Pablo Casals dinner at the White House in November, 1961, at which you were served very good drinks first; where there were ashtrays every-where just inviting you to poison yourself with cigarettes; where the line is formed alphabet-ically; and where, when you do line up, you are in a less querulous mood than otherwise because you have a drink and a cigarette; where, when the moment comes for you to greet the President and the First Lady, two ravishing people appear in the doorway who couldn't be more charming if they tried, who made you feel utterly welcome, even with a huge gathering. You are then brought in to dinner. Dinner turns out to be not at a horseshoe table but many little tables, seating about ten peo-ple apiece, fires roaring in all the fireplaces, and these tables are laid in three adjacent rooms so that it's all like having dinner with friends. The food is marvelous, the wines are delicious. . . . People are laughing, *laughing out loud*, telling sto-ries, jokes, enjoying themselves, glad to be there.

"I'll never forget the end of that evening when there was dancing. The marine band was playing waltzes or something, and Roy Harris and Walter Piston and people like that were kicking up their heels in the White House, a little high, just so de-lighted to be there, so glad that they had been asked, feeling that they had finally been recog-nized as honored artists of the Republic. You know, I've never seen so many happy artists in my life. It was a joy to watch it. And the feeling of hos-pitality, of warmth, of welcome, the taste with which everything was done. The goodness of ev-erything; it was just good. The guests were so in-teresting, and most of all the President and Mrs. Kennedy. It was like a different world, utterly like a different planet. I couldn't believe that this was the same White House that I had attended a year or so before and performed in."

Leonard Bernstein thought he had an appreciative audience in Caroline when they both watched him conduct a symphony on television. He was mistaken.

Bernstein had been invited to a dinner at the White House honoring the composer Igor Stravinsky. The concert he had taped earlier was scheduled for airing at eight P.M. When the time neared, he told Jackie he was anxious to see at least part of it and asked where he could find a television set. She told him there was one in Caroline's room.

"I sat with Caroline and her nurse, Maude Shaw, watching this thing," Bernstein said, "and I remember very well Caroline sitting, as I thought, hypnotized by this program and just thrilled with every moment and every note." Bernstein was particularly pleased because on Saturday mornings he gave concert-lectures to young people and had been highly praised as a musical educator.

Caroline brought him back to earth with a thud. Turning to him when the music paused, she gave her only comment: "I have my own horse." Deflated, the eminent conductor returned to the dinner party.

The guest list for the Senate dinner for André Malraux, the French Minister of Culture, in May, 1962, was again a gathering of the great and famous. It included Charles and Anne Lindbergh, painter Andrew Wyeth, poet Robert Lowell, playwrights Arthur Miller and Tennessee Williams, choreographer George Balanchine, and actress Geraldine Page.

Kennedy enjoyed these events hugely, commenting facetiously in his remarks that "this is becoming a sort of eating place for artists but they never ask us out."

J.F.K. was not above pulling an "Inspector Clousseau" once in a while, especially during his early days in the White House. At his first state luncheon on February 14, 1961, the President, after greeting his honored guests upstairs in the Oval Room, walked with them from the elevator directly to the Blue Room — or so he thought.

"Oh, this is another room I wanted to show you," he said calmly to his visitors, as he deftly backed out of the pantry.

After he moved into the White House, Kennedy discovered a flaw in the design that caused him and his guests some moments of discomfort. The Sunday after he was sworn in, Jackie gave a small dinner party for a few old friends. The guests were Franklin Delano Roosevelt, Jr., and his wife, newspaper columnist Joseph Alsop, artist William Walton, and Mary Russell, widow of a Washington journalist.

Following dinner in the family dining room, then on the first floor of the mansion, the ladies settled down for coffee and the gentlemen went on a hunt for a bathroom. In vain. They prevailed upon F.D.R., Jr., who, after all, had lived for years in the White House, but he couldn't remember where it was.

Finally, the three concluded that there was no bathroom on the first floor. Since the west wing, with the President's office, was too far away, they had to go to the family quarters on the second floor.

Strictly Personal

Jack Kennedy drank little because of recurring stomach problems. Before his election to the Presidency he went to nightclubs to watch the shows and gossip with and about celebrities, but he would nurse a single daiquiri all evening. In the White House he switched to a small Scotch with water, and sometimes drank Dom Perignon champagne. He liked an occasional glass of imported beer.

He avoided almost everything but the simplest and blandest dishes. He was a problem for hostesses who would prepare the most elaborate meals, which he would leave almost untouched. He preferred a hearty fish chowder, a fish casserole, beef Stroganoff, and great quantities of ice cream with chocolate sauce and milk. For breakfast he would have two four-and-one-half-minute boiled eggs, toast, several slices of broiled bacon, and coffee.

Following the lead of his brother Joe, he acquired a taste for strong black cigars. In turn, Bobby and Ted also became cigar smokers, but none of the brothers smoked cigarettes.

Kennedy never followed the crowd, not even in clothing styles. *Gentlemen's Quarterly,* the leading publication for men's fashions, noted that despite his social background, which called for the traditional Ivy League three-button jacket, he wore two-button single-breasted suits because he believed they were more flattering to him. The suits, with their long lapel rolls and open fronts, soon set a fashion trend across the country for men.

Because of his broad shoulders, J.F.K.'s suits needed little padding. He wore a size 40, but his 33-inch waist and slim hips required tapering in the hip area. He preferred trousers with no pleats, and only slightly tapering. His jackets were either vented in the center or had no vents at all, with sleeves short enough to permit about an inch of shirt cuff to show. He always selected dark — gray or blue — fabrics, either faintly striped or solid, never flannel or tweed, always worsted.

Nothing he wore was flamboyant. Ties were conservative, with stripes or small figures, always worn with a PT 109 clasp; sport jackets were quiet blues, tans, or grays, occasionally a classic tweed.

Said *Gentlemen's Quarterly*: "Because of his eminent position, his athletic build, and commanding appearance, and because he has exercised flexibility and good taste rather than follow slavish conformity, the President will continue to exert a salutary influence on the dress habits of American men."

The President had an astonishing memory for facts and figures and could quote long excerpts from books, studies, and reports, but was always losing topcoats, briefcases, and other personal effects. His secretary spent many hours of each week during his Senate years calling hotels, airlines, and terminals to determine the whereabouts of John F. Kennedy's possessions. In 1956, he misplaced his wallet at the Democratic convention in Chicago and it was never recovered. Kennedy was upset not because of the money — there were only a couple of dollars, Jackie said — but because it contained an air-travel card, his driver's license, and Jackie's gift of a Saint Christopher medal.

Several friends commented on his awareness that his life-span might be short. They detected a special urge to accomplish everything he could in the time allotted to him. George Smathers recalls an observation Jack made one day in Palm Beach after his spinal surgery. While Smathers was changing the bandage, he saw a hole in Kennedy's back that revealed the metal plate surgeons had inserted to keep his spine rigid. He remarked that Jack must be in great pain.

"I don't have time to worry about the hurt," said Kennedy, according to Jack Anderson. "I don't have time to be immobilized. We are here only a short time. I'm not going to sit out my life shivering and thinking about the hurt and the risk. I love the game of life. I'm going to jump back into it and scramble through as well as I can or die trying."

Kay Halle also observed that he had a sense that "perhaps he was not going to have as long a time as he might wish to do all he wanted to do." She added, "There was a curious sense in him that every moment seemed keenly important, and was not to be wasted."

Jackie may not have learned much about politics and politicians from her husband, but the President absorbed a good deal about fashion from his wife.

Princess Grace of Monaco lunched at the White House one day and was chatting with the President and other guests when he suddenly turned to her and asked, "Is that a Givenchy you're wearing?"

Startled, Grace looked down at her dress and asked, "However did you know, Mr. President?"

"Oh, I'm getting pretty good at it," Kennedy answered with a broad grin, "now that fashion is becoming more important than politics and the press is paying more attention to Jackie's clothes than to my speeches."

North Ocean Boulevard, or Route A1A on which the family's winter home is located, is a scenic highway skirting the Atlantic, only two lanes wide in the Palm Beach area. As President-elect, weary after lengthy conferences on his new program, J.F.K. told his aides he was going to take a spin on the road. He stepped into his car and swung onto the highway.

He raced along, rounding turns on squealing tires, with alarmed Secret Service men following. Kennedy, seeing that he was being tailed, drove faster. The chase lasted for dozens of miles until the Secret Service car managed to get him to brake. Agents poured out of their car and suggested he ought not to be so reckless.

Word was sent to Washington that day, and soon after a car with chauffeur was assigned to stand by and take the President-elect on drives along the ocean, or wherever he wanted to go.

Said Senator Smathers after the incident, "One reason I voted for Kennedy was to get him off the highways."

Distinguished visitors walked through the office of Evelyn Lincoln, Kennedy's personal secretary, when they came to see the President. One day J.F.K. suggested it might be "nice" if she stood up whenever a high-ranking personage entered. The following day, when he arrived for work, Mrs. Lincoln rose from her desk. The President asked her why she was standing. When she replied that a "dignitary" had just entered, he stared at her in puzzlement. Then, remembering, he laughed and told her to sit down.

Kennedy read everything. James A. Reed, Assistant Secretary of the Treasury and a friend since navy days, once presented him with an autographed copy of a book by Thornton W. Burgess, who wrote animal stories for children. Said Reed, "Whenever a book or a piece of paper or a magazine was presented to him, he would always become immediately engrossed in it—and he began to read *The Adventures of Reddy Fox*. There he was, the President of the United States, rocking in his rocking chair, reading the bedtime story that had been a favorite of his when he was a small boy."

Commenting on his voracious appetite for the printed word, Kennedy once lamented, "I made two mistakes during my first year: one was Cuba, and the other was letting it be known that I read as much as I do."

Kennedy enjoyed meeting with, and tilting verbal lances with, journalists, who liked him but did not spare him when they believed he merited criticism. Unlike some other Presidents, who asked for brief summaries of press accounts, Jack went through everything that was written, wincing often. "I'm reading more," he remarked wryly, "and enjoying it less."

A story made the rounds that Kennedy agreed to support the food-stamp program only if the color of the stamps would be changed from blue-and-orange to gold-and-Irish-green. After all, it was said, would an Irish Catholic want to be associated with Orangemen, members of the society that was founded to define Protestant interests in Northern Ireland?

When he won a bet he insisted on being paid promptly. On Saturday, November 22, just before his departure for Dallas, he made a bet with Dave Powers on the Duke-Navy football game. With a few others, the President listened to the game while lounging at the pool in his Palm Beach home. Powers' team lost and Jack wanted his money at once. Dave, clad in bathing attire, protested that he'd give it to him later when he got dressed, but Jack wouldn't listen. "Pay up," he demanded. And Powers did, going into the house and fetching the small amount of cash from his pants pocket. Jack stuck it into his trunks and grinned contentedly.

He liked mind exercises, intellectual puzzles, and especially word games. At various times, Chinese checkers and backgammon topped his list of cerebral encounters. Jack's favorite was called "Categories." It is played with a 25-box grid, in 5-X-5 format. Along the top above the grid are the categories Statesmen, Military Leaders, Foreign Cities, or whatever the players agree on. Down the left side are written five random letters of the alphabet. The object: to fill in the boxes with names in each category that begin with the letters on the left. The challenge: a five-minute time limit. The player who fills in the most boxes wins.

While all the Kennedys played this game, roughly from 1953 to 1956, Jack was the recognized champion.

The official Kennedy Presidential portrait was framed and hung in thousands of post offices, all army, navy, and air force installations, every government building, countless schools, and nobody knows how many private homes.

But that familiar full-face photo of an unsmiling J.F.K. in a dark pinstripe suit, his hair uncharacteristically neatly combed, was not that of a President at all! It was actually taken in his office the summer before his election, while he was still a senator. Kennedy personally chose this picture, which was taken in ten minutes by Fabian Bachrach of the Bachrach Photography Studios.

Leonard Lyons, the late syndicated columnist, wrote to J.F.K. that George Washington's autograph was selling for $175, Franklin D. Roosevelt's for $75, but J.F.K.'s was fetching only $65.

Replying by letter, Kennedy said he appreciated the information about the current state of the market for Kennedy signatures. Therefore, he added, in order not to depress the price still more, he would not sign this letter.

And he didn't.

On June 8, 1963, Kennedy addressed the women's division of the California State Central Committee at a breakfast meeting in Hollywood. He told them, "Looking at all you ladies and seeing what you have done with some of your distinguished officeholders, I recall an experience of the suffragettes who picketed the White House back during the First World War. The leader of the suffragettes was arrested. As she was taken away in a truck, she turned to her girls and said, "Don't worry, girls. Pray to the Lord. She will protect you."

Kennedy's private vocabulary was liberally strewn with three-, four- and five-letter-word obscenities.

A person he didn't like was a "prick"; someone who flopped on a job "fell on his ass"; he employed the f-word as a noun or adjective, sometimes both in one sentence. Lyndon Johnson was also a master cusser. One of his favorite expressions describing people who, he felt, didn't know as much about a subject as he thought they should, was: "He doesn't know his ass from his elbow."

John Kenneth Galbraith, J.F.K.'s friend and ambassador to India during the Kennedy administration, said of the two, "In private, Kennedy often uttered four-letter words, which was considered part of his charm; when Johnson used the same words he was described as vulgar."

Gene Schoor, the author, was in the White House interviewing Kennedy for a biography for young people. Kennedy confided he was in severe pain. "Everyday," he said, "I'm lucky to get out of bed." After a while, Jack asked Schoor to accompany him to the dispensary on the basement floor, where he would get an injection of novocaine for his back, which helped numb the physical distress.

Schoor, a former boxer, had the beginnings of a paunch. Pointing to it as they left the Oval Office, Kennedy observed, "For an ex-boxer, you're in fucking lousy shape."

Sympathetically but candidly, the writer replied, "Mr. President, you're not in such fucking great shape yourself."

En route to and from official functions, Jack always strode ahead of his wife, a fact that was noticed by Americans and prompted more than 400 letters daily. "Impolite," "ungentlemanly," and "discourteous" were some of the criticisms leveled at the President.

When Pierre Salinger told him he was arousing adverse comment, Kennedy replied, "Jackie will just have to walk faster."

Judy Garland's voice enraptured the President. On several occasions he called her from the Oval Office and asked her to sing "Over The Rainbow" to him. The work of the Presidency halted as John Kennedy leaned back at his desk, closed his eyes, and listened as Judy sang.

From his Oval Office he could walk out under a colonnade supported by white pillars into the Rose Garden, where the first blooms were planted in 1913 by Ellen Axson Wilson. Traditionally, Presidents have welcomed heads of state and other foreign dignitaries in this lovely area, where planting beds frame a broad lawn.

The roses and other flowers in the beds were carefully tended and bloomed prettily, but the lawn usually looked about the same as those in front of many suburban homes — browning out in spots, bare in others. The President groused that distinguished visitors would get a poor impression of the place. When repeated efforts by White House gardeners failed to produce a lush, green lawn, he came up with a solution.

He ordered green paint to be sprayed on the barren spots whenever the schedule called for a top-level personage to be greeted in the garden.

When Kennedy's back was acting up, tossing a baseball was painful. But each April, when the Washington Senators began their season, the President had to throw out the first ball. Concerned that he might appear less than proficient in his ceremonial pitches, he would slip out of the

Oval Office days ahead of time and practice by throwing softballs in the Rose Garden.

It paid off. When the 1961 season opened, Kennedy hurled the ball twice, both times fully ninety feet. Baseball statisticians do not compile records of Presidential pitches, but, according to *The New York Times,* "observers were sure they [Kennedy's pitches] probably set a record."

They may have been great pitches, but they didn't help the home team. The Chicago White Sox beat the Senators, 4–3.

Salinger was a favorite target of Jack's barbs and practical jokes. The Fifty-Mile Hike stands as a monument to the President's ribbing of his corpulent secretary and to his persistence in carrying a joke as far as it could go.

The subject was fitness, which the Kennedy administration elevated almost to a religion. In February, 1963, a letter came to Jack's attention indicating that more than a half century before, Teddy Roosevelt had similar notions. Why couldn't officers of the United States Marine Corps, T. R. asked, take fifty-mile hikes every so often to set an example of fitness for the country?

J.F.K. bucked the letter to General David M. Shoup, the marine corps commandant, asking him to send it back to the White House as Shoup's discovery. "You might want to add a comment," he wrote, "that today's marine corps officers are just as fit as those of 1908, and are willing to improve it. I, in turn, will ask Mr. Salinger for a report on the fitness of the White House staff."

When Shoup's letter arrived, Kennedy handed it to Pierre, saying, "You realize, of course, that somebody from the White House will have to go down there and march with the marines."

Salinger began to sense something in the wind. "Why not Kenny O'Donnell?" he told Jack quickly. "He's always in great shape."

"No," the President said. "He should be somebody who needs the exercise, somebody who would be an inspiration to millions of other out-of-shape Americans."

Pierre paled visibly. The outlook was ominous.

Salinger, at thirty-seven, had a hearty appetite which, combined with lack of exercise, had caused his weight to balloon to 185 pounds, 20 more than he should be carrying. He put his fertile mind to squirming out of the deal, and the next day thought he found a way.

A *Washington Post* reporter had quoted Brigadier General Godfrey T. McHugh, Jr., Kennedy's air force aide, as saying it would be "loads of fun to go on a fifty-mile hike every day." Salinger rushed into the President's office with the story.

"All right," J.F.K. said, "you're off the hook. You can tell the press McHugh is our man." Salinger promptly issued a press communiqué saying that the President had noted the *Post* report and would consider it fitting if the general would go on the march with the marines.

McHugh, however, hit the ceiling. "I was misquoted by the Post," he fumed. "I am not a volunteer and I suspect Mr. Salinger of self-serving motives in announcing that I am. I have spoken to the President and he accepted my explanation of the matter."

It was a setback for Pierre, but J.F.K. had no sympathy. "I could have told you," he said, "that a civilian always loses when he tries to meddle with the military."

Salinger took a lot of needling from the White House reporters about his predicament. Gag gifts — crutches, a compass, corn plasters, bottles of liniment — poured into his office.

He took revenge. At one afternoon press briefing, Salinger suggested that he would be guilty of suppressing the news if he didn't insist on full coverage of the hike. He let the press know that he expected all White House reporters to do the same fifty miles.

"When I walk, everybody walks," he said.

The newsmen started to worry. "Pierre," one reporter asked, "do you actually see any real and present danger of this hiking gag escalating into the real thing?"

"I think there is every possibility it will," Salinger responded.

"Mr. Secretary, may I ask you a personal question? How far did you go for lunch today?"

"I went to the Jockey Club — by automobile."

"You're exhausting my physical fitness," said one of the reporters.

"Pierre, in the Civil War you could buy a volunteer to take our place," advised another.

"I cannot permit that. We are all in over our heads."

"Can you arrange to have some of those Saint Bernard dogs that carry little flasks around their necks?"

"Austerity is going to be our motto," Salinger shot back.

"How long do you think the hike will last?"

"Up to three days."

"Oh, shit!"

The Sunday before the big event, Bobby Kennedy, accompanied by three friends, began a fifty-mile hike from the Chesapeake and Ohio Canal at Chain Bridge to Camp David, the Presidential retreat. Assembling before dawn were Edwin Guthman, his press officer; David Hackett, whom he knew from prep-school days, and James Symington, son of Senator Stuart Symington. The four set off in twelve-degree cold.

At the halfway mark, the small group sat on the frozen ground. Guthman and Hackett, both former athletes, Hackett a football star, said they couldn't go on.

Wearily, Bobby rose and continued along, calling back mournfully, "Your brother isn't President of the United States."

If Guthman and Hackett couldn't make it, and lean, tough, Bobby barely did, Pierre foresaw disaster for himself if he tried, and so informed the President. "Well," J.F.K. said finally, "if you can't, you can't. But you're going to have to come up with a good reason."

Pierre was ingenious. On Tuesday, with only three days to go, he got Dick Snider, administrator of the President's Council on Physical Fitness, to issue a statement saying that fifty-mile hikes were not a good idea for everyone and advising unfit people against such an undertaking.

In his account of his years with the President, *With Kennedy,* Pierre said forthrightly, "The council gave its advice to the nation at eleven and I took it at twelve."

At his press briefing that noontime, Pierre cited the fitness council's statement warning that people who were not in good shape should not attempt fifty-mile hikes.

"And," he concluded, "my shape is not good."

Continuing, he invoked Bobby Kennedy. "I believe the fitness of this administration has already been amply demonstrated by the Attorney General. A further demonstration on my part would be superfluous and possibly disastrous. I am therefore rescinding the hike previously announced.

"I may be plucky, but I am not stupid."

Later, Pierre received an engraved calendar from General Shoup with the dates of the crisis raised and an inscription saying that while some Cabinets may have better legs, "your footwork is superb."

Representative Hale Boggs of Louisiana, the Democratic whip who attended weekly meetings with the President and was in close touch with him throughout his administration, made this evaluation of the man in an oral history for the Kennedy Library. It is a simple, clear summing-up of the President's approach to governing the nation:

"He was able to carry on a political dialogue which was as sophisticated and as mature as anything we have ever had in this country. And this was what was so tragic about those people who misunderstood the man. This man did more for the maturing of political thought in America than any man in modern times, in my judgment, and yet the people who harbored these strong emotions against him fail to understand that completely, as I see it.

"His whole effort was to temper conditions, to overcome disagreement, to unite the nation. This is why he took so long to come out with a civil rights bill. He had a thorough understanding of the difficulties that confronted the smaller Southern communities, and so on. He understood this perfectly. His whole approach was one of understanding and sympathy, and yet, once he had decided on a course of action, he never hesitated."

Chapter Eight

Foreign Crises

The New Frontier got off to a fast start. On January 21, the day after the inauguration, Kennedy issued his first executive order, doubling the amount of food distributed by the American government to impoverished families. Four days later he permitted the first live telecast of a Presidential press conference, at which he announced the release from Russian prison of two American fliers shot down over Soviet territory. During his first State of the Union address, on January 29, Kennedy announced plans for a Peace Corps and a Food for Peace program, both designed to aid Latin-American countries.

His first major crisis came on April 17 with the landing of the 1,400 Cuban-refugee army at Zapata Bay, only to be crushed in less than three days by Castro's troops. Kennedy, who had inherited the plan from the previous administration, nevertheless accepted the responsibility for allowing it to proceed.

In mid-May, he made his first foreign trip to Canada, where he addressed the Canadian Parliament and hurt his back again, wielding a shovel during a tree-planting ceremony. On May 31, he and Jackie went to Paris, where he conferred with Charles de Gaulle about problems in Berlin and Southwest Asia, and Jackie entranced the Parisians. Then for two days the Kennedys went to Vienna, where he met with Nikita Khrushchev, the Soviet premier, who told the President he intended to sign a peace treaty with East Germany that year. Khrushchev hinted this would result in the closing of access routes to West Berlin.

Two months later, on August 13, the Russians erected a wall of barbed wire, concrete pillars, and stone blocks, separating East and West Berlin and preventing the passage from one sector to the other.

The most serious incident of Kennedy's administration occurred in October, 1962, when the Russians in Cuba began secretly installing 66 missiles capable of hurling nuclear warheads, 24 with a range of 1,100 miles, and 42 with a 2,200 mile range. The weapons could easily destroy Washington, New York, and Philadelphia; they could pulverize Chicago, Kansas City, and reach as far as Denver. This Cuban Missile Crisis, defused after thirteen harrowing days, brought the world closer than it had ever been before or since to nuclear war.

After the missile crisis, Kennedy struggled to get the U.S.S.R. to sign the first disarmament treaty since the nuclear era began. In June, 1963, he said, "If we cannot end now all our differences, at least we can help make the world safe for diversity. For . . . we all inhabit this small planet. We all breathe the same air. We all cherish our children's future. And we are all mortal." Averell Harriman ultimately got Russia to agree to a ban on testing nuclear weapons above ground and in the water. On September 24, 1963, the Senate ratified the treaty, which was signed on October 7.

In June of that year, Kennedy undertook a ten-day tour of Europe, which turned out to be the last foreign trip of his Presidency.

Troubles in Cuba and Asia

Less than three months after he took office, Jack Kennedy suffered a humiliating defeat in Cuba. The invasion he authorized to topple Fidel Castro was planned so badly and carried out so ineptly that a crushing defeat at the hands of over-whelmingly superior forces was all but inevitable.

Of the 1,400 Cuban emigrés in the invading force, fewer than one-tenth were trained soldiers. The others were drawn from civilian occupations, ranging from clerks and teachers to bankers, doctors, and musicians. Many were in their forties and fifties; some were in their sixties. The newest recruits had only the most rudimentary acquaintance with a rifle.

It was an incredible tragedy of errors. The troops had been instructed to "melt into the hills" after landing, but weren't informed — because their C.I.A. instructors did not know themselves! — that the closest hills were about 75 miles from the beach, accessible only by wading through swampland.

Many landing craft were ripped apart by under-water coral reefs they didn't know, and were not told, were lying there. Those who made it to shore were outnumbered and outgunned by government troops, estimated at 100,000 men, led by Castro himself. Abandoned by the United States, which provided no air support, the exiles were pushed into the sea, where there were no rescue ships to remove them. The 1,200 survivors who escaped the strafing by 122-millimeter howitzers, supplied by Russia, surrendered.

The plan to invade Cuba, a C.I.A. project, had begun during Ike's administration. Kennedy could have stopped it cold but was convinced by Allan Dulles, the C.I.A. head whom he admired, and most of his Cabinet that it could work.

It was a terrible time for Jack Kennedy and perhaps even worse for Bobby, who bled every time his brother was hurt. Bobby cried after the debacle, telling Jack, "Those black-bearded communists can't do this to you." Jack was close to tears himself.

Observing his chief's drawn features and lackluster eyes, Dave Powers said of the incident, "That's the first thing he ever really lost."

Kenny O'Donnell, who came from a middle-class family, was not accustomed to formal wear and skipped any White House event to which he was invited where he'd have to don tails. The annual congressional reception was held on Tuesday evening, April 18, the day after the invasion. Jack told him, "I want you there," and Kenny, muttering, went out to rent white tie and tails. He wandered around the East Room, still grumbling, in his ill-fitted suit, watching the President chatting easily with the guests.

Lester David and Irene David

Soon after the reception began, Major General Chester V. (Ted) Clifton, Kenny's military aide, told Kenny the President wanted to handle the incoming calls in the Oval Office. Kenny sat in the Presidential chair and began to receive bulletins about the rapidly deteriorating situation. Walt W. Rostow, deputy aide for national security affairs, told him, "The operation is going in the shit house," and urged him to arrange an emergency meeting in the White House when the reception ended.

It was an extraordinary post-midnight session that lasted almost three hours. Kennedy, Vice-President Johnson, Secretary of State Dean Rusk, Defense Secretary Robert S. McNamara, and Kenny were wearing their tails, and the military and naval chiefs were in beribboned dress uniforms.

More and more dismal news poured in from the beachhead. Admiral Burke pleaded with Jack to let him use jet planes from the aircraft carrier *Essex* to down Castro's aircraft. Kennedy refused. Nor would he allow a destroyer to be sent in to blast Castro's tanks. "I don't want the United States involved in this," Kennedy insisted, saying over and over that it was an operation conducted by Cuban patriots.

By three A.M. nothing had been resolved. The news got worse. The President sat silently. Then at about four he rose, opened the white-curtained French doors, and walked out into the Rose Garden. The temperature hovered around fifty. Spring shoots were just starting to appear in the President's Park, on the south grounds of the White House. Kennedy did not see them in the darkness as he walked for almost an hour on the paths.

Historian Arthur Schlesinger, Jr., had written Kennedy two memos, one on April 5 and another only a week prior to the invasion, explaining why it should not be attempted. Wryly, Jack told aides that Schlesinger had better not include those notes in any book while he (Kennedy) was still alive. He offered a title to Schlesinger, nonetheless: *Kennedy: The Only Years*.

What went wrong? A six-week investigation by a board of inquiry, headed by General Maxwell Taylor, came up with some complex answers, but here is Jack Kennedy's own no-frills explanation, as recorded in an Oral History by Jack Bell, the Associated Press correspondent:

> This [The Bay of Pigs debacle] was a real gloomy time around Washington. I asked Jack about this one day. "Just what did happen? How did you get yourself in this mess?"
>
> "Well," he said, "you know, I believe the things I'd read in the magazines about all these people in government. I'd been reading a lot about them. I didn't really know them. I didn't know how good they were, but everything I read said they were tremendous." Then he said, "Arleigh Burke* came in, sat down by my desk. I said, 'Will this thing work?' He said, 'As far as we have been able to check it out, this is fine. The plan is good.'
>
> "Hell, I'd been reading about 'Thirty Knot' Burke for a long time. I thought he

was tremendous. Allen Dulles came in. He sat in a chair right over there, and told me all about this plan, what had been done. You know, he sat there, and he said, 'I'm more confident that this will succeed than I ever was about the Guatemalan thing.**'" Kennedy said, "What do you do in a case like that? I looked at all this, and it didn't look good. But look at the advice I had." I said to him, "Go ahead." He said, "I did. It wasn't anybody else's fault. It was mine. I couldn't judge the people I got the advice from.'"

Logically, one would expect that the administration's disastrous failure in the Bay of Pigs would have plummeted John Kennedy's standing in the Presidential approval polls. But the American public, as politicians have discovered over the years, does not heed the rules of logic. Two weeks after the fiasco, J.F.K.'s rating blipped upward.

Reading the newest poll results, Jack observed wryly, "It's just like Eisenhower. The worse I do, the more popular I get."

The Bay of Pigs debacle, spread across the front pages and monopolizing the TV and radio news

---

*Admiral Arleigh Burke, chief of naval operations, achieved fame because of the speed with which he was able to move his squadrons during World War II.

**In 1954, the C.I.A. backed an anti-communist coup against the Guatemalan regime, headed by Jacobo Arbenz. The revolt succeeded and Castillo Armas was installed in his place. The C.I.A. had hoped to duplicate the success in Cuba.

broadcasts, obscured for a time the rapidly worsening situation in Southeast Asia.

Laos and Vietnam were locked in an ideological struggle between pro-Western and communist forces. In Laos, once a part of French Indochina, a civil war was raging. The anti-communist premier, Boun Oum, was opposed by Prince Souphanouvong, who was backed by the insurgent Pathet Lao, a group of tribal chiefs supported by the communists. Complicating the problem was a third group, headed by Souvanna Phouma, which advocated a policy of neutrality between East and West.

A few weeks after Kennedy was inaugurated, the Pathet Lao was almost at the gates of Vientiane, the Laotian capital. The new President faced a tough choice: Should U.S. Marines be flown in to prevent the small, but strategic country from toppling to the communists? Should he do nothing and hope for the best? Could the marines stop the communists if they did arrive? Did they know the terrain well enough? Could they match the mountain tribesmen there who knew that kind of warfare so much better?

Kennedy compromised. He ordered marines into friendly Thailand, and placed naval forces on alert in the China Sea. By mid-year, the administration won an agreement for a cease-fire in Laos, but it didn't last long. The Pathet Lao's offensive resumed.

Laos was only part of the problem in Southeast Asia. Seven years earlier, after the Indochina War, the country of Vietnam to the east, an area the size of Wyoming, had been split into Tonkin in the

northern section, Cochin China in the south, and
Annam in the center. Ho Chi Minh, a communist,
emerged as leader in the north, determined to
bring the entire country under red domination.

It was no secret in Washington that Russia was
supplying both the Pathet Lao and Ho Chi Minh's
communist Vietnimh, and that Ho's jungle
fighters were infiltrating into the south — which
had been established as a republic — by way of
Laos.

In the southern area, which had become known
as South Vietnam, President Ngo Dinh Diem was
host to every important American official who
came to visit. He fed them sumptuous banquets
in his Saigon palace—and put the arm on each for
help. He warned them over and over that unless
U.S. troops were sent to beef up his defenses, he
could not hold back the communists, who would
then eventually control all of Southeast Asia.

But Kennedy would not commit any more men
to Vietnam than the 685 "advisers" already there.
In October, he sent two of his most trusted aides,
General Maxwell Taylor and Walt Rostow, to
Saigon to study the situation. The bottom line of
their findings: America *should* send troops to prevent a communist victory.

Still the President hesitated. He told Arthur
Schlesinger in the White House that troops would
be greeted with an ovation but "in four days" few
would remember. "Then we will be told we have
to send in more troops," he said. "It's like taking a
drink. The effect wears off, and you have to take
another."

Nobody could understand why the Vietnam exercise turned out the way it did. John Kennedy knew the dangers of engaging in a war with guerrillas who fought on their own jungle terrain. He had taken to heart Charles de Gaulle's warning at the Elyseé Palace that Westerners could not win a land war in that part of the world. De Gaulle spoke from painful experience. The 1954 French defeat at Dien Bien Phu lost the war in Indochina at a cost of 253 casualties and $4,000,000,000. General Douglas MacArthur had told him, too, that the number of Asian warriors available to do battle was limitless, far greater than America could provide. And topping everything else, Kennedy had little faith in the accuracy of information provided to him by our foreign service.

Why, then, were there 16,732 Americans in Vietnam in the closing months of 1963? In his Oral History, Bobby was at a loss for an answer. He said, "I don't know what would be best — to say that he didn't spend much time thinking about Vietnam, or to say that he did and messed it up."

His brother's sharp escalation of America's involvement in Vietnam created for Bobby one of the worst dilemmas of his political career. A hawk throughout 1962 and 1963 — he kept a green beret on his desk at the Department of Justice — he turned dove by the end of 1964.

For months he wrestled with the question: How could he disavow the policies of his dead brother and his own earlier arguments that the war must be fought hard and won? As the casualties mounted and the suffering of the Vietnamese worsened, Bobby's internal emotional tug-of-war continued. "Facing it was an everyday agony for him," declared Harris Wofford.

After his return from a tour of Southeast Asia in 1967, Bobby made up his mind to speak out. He wrote a forceful, emotional speech and asked his old friend Senator Fred R. Harris of Oklahoma, who lived nearby, to come and hear it. Harris and his wife, LaDonna, came to Hickory Hill, where, over coffee and chocolate cake, Bobby read his talk.

He had finally come to terms with breaking with his brother's policies, he explained, but another doubt was assailing him. Now a senator from New York, he wondered if people would think his opposition to the war was politically motivated. Would the country believe he was using his stand, which disagreed totally with President Lyndon Johnson, as a springboard to the Presidency in 1968?

Harris told him, "You have to do what you think is right. Go ahead and make the speech." LaDonna agreed.

Bobby looked relieved. The Harrises finished their coffee but found their cake plates empty. Brumus, Bobby's huge black Newfoundland, had gone from one plate to another, gobbling their portions and licking the plates clean. Bobby liked chocolate cake. So did Brumus.

European Tourists

The Paris and Vienna visits that first spring were intended to meet and size up two powerful heads of states, de Gaulle of France and Khrushchev of the Soviet Union. Kennedy felt that the advice of his diplomats concerning the two leaders' characters, personalities, and goals was secondhand. He wanted to see and judge for himself.

On the morning of May 31, slightly ahead of schedule, Air Force One arrived at Orly Field in Paris, where the President and Mrs. Kennedy were welcomed by General and Madame de Gaulle, United States ambassador to France James Gavin, and Hervé Alphand, the French ambassador to the United States. To the roll of drums and the strains of "The Star-Spangled Banner" and "La Marseillaise," the dour, aging de Gaulle and the handsome young American President traversed a 75-yard red carpet to the Salon d'Honneur for the formal welcoming speeches.

Half a million persons jammed a 10-mile route waving banners (including one from Harvard), cheering and jockeying for a glimpse of Jackie, beauteous in a blue Oleg Cassini coat and pillbox hat. Leading the motorcade were a phalanx of 50 police on motorcycles and members of the Garde Républicain on horseback, all of whom accompanied the party to the elegant Palais des Affaires Etrangères at the Quai d'Orsay, reserved by the French government for top-level personages.

Kennedy was accustomed to luxurious surroundings, but these floored him. He and Jackie had separate, vast three-room apartments, across the hall from each other, he in the Louis XVI bedroom, which was paneled in blue-gray silk, and she in La Chambre de la Reine, recently occupied by Queen Fabiola of Belgium.

As soon as J.F.K. entered his quarters, he made a beeline for the bathtub to soak his aching back. It was about a dozen feet long and half that in width, and was plated in pure gold.

"Maybe it's a better use for gold," he observed, "than locking it up at Fort Knox."

The visit blended serious talk and pageantry. Kennedy and de Gaulle conferred for six sessions, alone and with advisers, on a wide range of topics that included Berlin, Laos, the North Atlantic Treaty Organization, and nuclear energy. With de Gaulle, J.F.K. laid a wreath on the tomb of the Unknown Soldier beneath the Arc de Triomphe at the end of the Champs Élysées. He went to the United States embassy, where he told employees there that "I tried to be assigned to the embassy in Paris myself, and unable to do so, I decided I would run for President."

Jackie stopped traffic wherever she went, and the press wrote glowingly about her beauty, her charm, and her clothes. She tried to be diplomatic in her choice of designers. For a formal dinner for 1,000 the first night at the Élysée Palace, she selected one of American-born Cassini's designs, a dazzling gown that bared one shoulder. The next night, however, for the dinner at the Versailles Palace, she wore an elegant white satin gown with a bodice of red, white and blue, a creation of famed French designer Hubert de Givenchy.

That Versailles dinner was the stuff of fairy tales. It was held in the candlelit Hall of Mirrors, and the sumptuous feast was brought out on gold-trimmed china that had belonged to Napoleon. After watching a performance of the French ballet, the Kennedys ended the evening with a stroll through the moonlit gardens, shepherded by de Gaulle.

Jackie all but stole the show during the visit. She captivated de Gaulle, who couldn't take his eyes off her at official luncheons and at the Versailles dinner. The year before, the French president had observed, following his visit to the U.S., "If there were anything I could take back to France with me, it would be Mrs. Kennedy." The newspapers couldn't publish enough photographs, the crowds couldn't shout loud enough when she passed.

Her husband was impressed. He introduced himself at a press conference of French, British, and American journalists with one of his most-quoted lines: "I," he said, "am the man who accompanied Jacqueline Kennedy to Paris."

The two days of talks that followed in Vienna with Khrushchev on June 3 and 4 were tough and un-compromising. Kennedy, in excruciating pain since the tree-planting ceremony at Ottawa's Gov-ernment House, was forced to use crutches, which he discarded when he appeared in public. The cold war turned icy as the two leaders confer-red in private, first at the American embassy resi-dence in a suburb four miles from the city, then at the Soviet embassy in Vienna. Kennedy was calm, firm, logical; the stubby little Soviet premier was loud, blustery, and bullying, illustrating his points with colorful peasant vernacular.

A few light moments leavened the serious tone. At the American embassy, Kennedy lit a cigar and flipped the match in the direction of the chair in which Khrushchev was sitting.

The Russian, watching it arc downward, re-marked, a rare smile creasing his pudgy features, "Are you trying to set me on fire?"

Kennedy replied, also with a smile, that it was not his intention to burn the premier.

Whereupon, Khrushchev countered, "Aha! You're a capitalist, not an incendiary."

Two years earlier, the Soviet premier had caused a furor when, on his first visit to the U.S., he had boasted, "We will bury you." The remark was taken as a warning to capitalist countries by a bel-ligerent, avowed enemy. Later, Khrushchev ex-plained that he meant "burial" in an economic, not military, sense. During the Vienna summit, the First Secretary again said Russia would bury America, but this time few Americans knew about it.

In a conversation with Dean Rusk, Khrushchev, a miner's son, held forth on the subject of dwarf corn, asserting that it was not possible to grow the crop in any meaningful quantity. Rusk, reared on a Georgia farm, argued that it was indeed possible, and that when he returned to the States he would fly over some samples of the crop.

Khrushchev shifted gears. If America could grow dwarf corn in quantity, it was because she had superior farm equipment and fertilizer. If these would be available to Russian farmers, he said, the Soviet Union would bury the United States — in corn.

Khrushchev returned home from Vienna in a jubilant mood. In Moscow, he greeted Dr. Achmed Sukarno, president of the Republic of Indonesia, who was paying a state visit. At the official ceremonies, the premier presented Sukarno with an elegant automobile and a statue of a Soviet woman athlete. The following day, a party was held at the Indonesian embassy in honor of Sukarno's sixtieth birthday, an event Khrushchev noted with unrestrained hijinks.

At the sound of music, Khrushchev spotted Leonid Brezhnev, the fifty-eight-year-old dour Soviet president, standing next to Anastas Mikoyan, sixty-five, then the deputy premier. Shoving the two men toward each other, he bellowed, "Dance, you two!"

Nobody disobeys the First Secretary in the Soviet Union. Dutifully, Brezhnev pretended to be the female partner, while Mikoyan took the male role. Watching Mikoyan, who would later become chairman of the presidium of the Soviet Union, Khrushchev said, "He's a good dancer. That's why we keep him on the job." Brezhnev, of course, would soon succeed Khrushchev as premier. If both men were humiliated, they did not, or dared not, show it.

In the course of the evening, Nikita banged away at bongo drums, plunked himself in front of the orchestra, led it with a borrowed baton, and cavorted on the dance floor.

John Kennedy came home weary and depressed. "It was a very sober two days," John Kennedy told the American people on his return.

"The facts of the matter," he said in a report to the nation, "are that the Soviets and ourselves give wholly different meanings to the same words: war, peace, democracy, and popular will. We have wholly different views of right and wrong, of what is an internal affair and what is aggression. And above all, we have wholly different concepts of where the world is and where it is going. . . .

"Our most somber talks were on the subject of Germany and Berlin. I made it clear to Mr. Khrushchev that the security of Western Europe and therefore our own security are deeply involved in our presence and our access rights to West Berlin, that those rights are based on law, not on sufferance; and that we are determined to maintain those rights at any risk and thus our obligation to the people of West Berlin and their right to choose their own future. . . .

228

"Mr. Khrushchev did not talk in terms of war. He believes the world will move his way without resort to force. Most of all, he predicted the triumph of communism in the new and less-developed countries. He was certain that the tide there was moving his way, that the revolution of rising peoples would eventually be a communist revolution, and that the so-called wars of liberation supported by the Kremlin would replace the old methods of direct aggression.

"This is the communist theory. But I believe just as strongly that time will prove it wrong, that liberty and independence and self-determination, not communism, is the future of man. . . ."

"It's going to be a cold winter," he had told the Soviet premier after their final meeting. On the way home, he was steeped in despair, convinced that the tensions between the two superpowers were closer than ever to a flash point.

When he stretched out in his cabin on Air Force One to catch some sleep, a slip of paper fluttered to the floor. Evelyn Lincoln, his secretary, who accompanied him, picked it up along with other documents and began sorting the papers to make certain that classified material was safely stored away.

On it Kennedy had written these chilling words: "I know there is a God — and I see a storm coming; if He has a place for me, I believe I am ready."

The Wall

It wasn't a cold winter, but "a very hot summer," said Walt Rostow.

The overarching reason for Khrushchev's anger in Vienna — the "bone in our throat," he called it — was allied occupation rights in Berlin, where the western zone was administered by America, France, and Britain, the eastern zone by the U.S.S.R. West Berlin, an oasis of freedom surrounded by communist-dominated East Germany, was galling to the Russians. Daily, hundreds of Berliners were pulling up stakes and moving to the allied zone, a people-hemorrhage that worsened and soon threatened to deplete the lifeblood of the communist area.

Infuriated, Khrushchev threatened to sign a separate peace treaty with East Germany that would give Russia control over the entire city. At Vienna, Kennedy had tried to dissuade him from the rash step, which would not be tolerated by the allies and would almost certainly trigger a war.

In the White House, an unsmiling John Kennedy told aides, "He thinks I have no guts." On June 25, he delivered a television address that sent shudders through the nation and the world. America did not want armed conflict, he declared, "but we have fought before." He said, "We cannot and will not permit the communists to drive us out of Berlin, either gradually or by force.

"For our fulfillment of our pledge to that city is essential to the morale and security of West Germany, to the unity of Western Europe, and to the faith of the entire Free World."

The President began putting the nation on war alert. He ordered draft calls doubled, then tripled; he boosted the strength of the combat forces by 217,000; he strengthened the West Berlin garrison; he ordered planes and ships that had been mothballed into active service; and he asked Congress to appropriate an additional $3,500,000,000 for defense.

What brought the war crisis closest to every home was Kennedy's somber call to Americans to build bomb shelters in the event of a nuclear assault. He told them, "In the event of an attack, the lives of those families which are not hit in a nuclear blast and fire can still be saved. If they can be warned to take shelter and if that shelter is available . . . the time to start is now."

Just before the speech, he talked to Paul (Red) Fay, the Undersecretary of the Navy. Usually his conversations with the affable Fay were filled with jokes and joshing; this time he was dead serious. Kennedy asked him if he had built his bomb shelter. "No," Red replied. "I built a swimming pool."

Kennedy's shuddery retort: "You made a mistake."

Homeowners who had already built shelters and wanted to sell their houses found themselves besieged by buyers willing to pay outrageous prices. Manufacturers of prefabricated shelters couldn't keep up with the demand. Most newspapers and magazines published detailed articles on how to construct them and, when completed, what to put into them.

Few, apparently, gave a thought to what kind of world they would find if they managed to survive an atomic blast.

Khrushchev was in deep trouble, and not only in Berlin. At home crops were poor or failing, and farm animals were succumbing to disease in alarming numbers. In a northern village near the Baltic Sea, according to one story, a communist bureaucrat castigated a farmer who reported the loss of a large number of pigs.

"What is the reason?," the farmer was asked. "So many pigs lost . . . how do you account for it?"

The farmer shook his head and raised both arms in a gesture of helplessness. "Comrade Chairman," he replied, "I'm just as puzzled as you are. The only thing I can think of is that they are committing suicide."

Kennedy knew what Khrushchev was facing. The first week in August, he and Walt Rostow walked along the colonnade between the executive mansion and the Oval Office. By then, more than 30,000 East Berliners, many of them professionals and skilled technicians, were fleeing to the West every month.

"Khrushchev is losing East Germany," Kennedy told Rostow. "He cannot let that happen. If East Germany goes, so will Poland and all of Eastern Europe."

Then came a remarkable forecast. "He will have to do something to stop the flow," J.F.K. continued — "perhaps a wall."

The next week the prophecy was fulfilled. Early Sunday morning, August 13, gangs of East Berlin workmen, guarded by armed troops, began stringing 28 miles of barbed wire along the border separating the Berlins and split the old city in half. By Thursday, construction of a brick-and-concrete wall was begun. Four weeks later, it cut a jagged line through the city, shutting the gate to freedom for the inhabitants.

People who worked in the free zone were unable to get to their jobs. Families were separated. There were heartbreaking scenes of young people standing on ladders and holding up their youngsters so that grandparents on the other side could see their grandchildren. A tearful couple who had planned a large wedding in the eastern zone was married before only a handful of guests. The rest of the family was locked on the other side.

John Kennedy had gone to Hyannis Port that weekend, attended mass on Sunday at St. Francis Xavier, the little white church where his family worshipped, and later went for a cruise on Nantucket Sound. It wasn't until late in the afternoon, while he was at sea, that he was informed of the developments.

By then, ten P.M. Berlin time, the barbed-wire prelude to the wall was well under way. The question must be asked: With the superpowers at flashpoint over Berlin, why wasn't the President informed earlier? It has never been answered.

In the evening, Kennedy telephoned McGeorge Bundy, his national security adviser, asking him, "Why didn't we know?"

Intelligence had failed utterly to get wind of Khrushchev's action. Why? An operation of that magnitude, involving thousands of workmen, troops and police, not to mention supplies of wire, brick, mortar, and cement, would be hard to keep secret.

Norman Gelb, who was in Berlin as chief European correspondent for the Mutual Broadcasting Network, points out: "Berlin was a city of spies, divided loyalties, and rumors. People were passing back and forth all the time. It was a situation in which confidentiality was virtually impossible to maintain. Yet the allies were caught totally, unqualifiedly by surprise."

The administration was stunned and confused. Mac Bundy mirrored everyone's feelings when, early the next morning, he sat disconsolately with Deputy C.I.A. Director Robert Amory and asked, "What the hell do we do now?"

The wall could not be knocked down, Kennedy said, because it was inside the Soviet zone, where Khrushchev could do what he wished. And if it were demolished by the allies, he asked, what would stop him from building another one deeper inside East Berlin?

Nobody could be sure what was in the premier's mind. Was the wall his first step in a move to seize West Berlin? Was he interested only in plugging up the people-leak into West Berlin, or would he try to block all the access roads across East Germany into the allied sectors?

As tension mounted, Kennedy ordered 1,500 fully armed troops to the wall, but with strict instructions to remain well inside the allied zone. On the other side, combat-ready Soviet tanks and two divisions of red troops were moved into position.

As it turned out, Khrushchev had won what he wanted; he had stemmed the flow of refugees to the West. He had no intention of starting a war with the allies and, the next day, withdrew his troops and tanks, and the crisis was over.

Kennedy's final trip outside the United States was intended to cement America's relationship with its European allies. On June 22, he flew to Cologne and then visited West Berlin, Ireland, Great Britain, Italy, and the Vatican. Enormous throngs greeted him wherever he went, but nowhere was the reception more fervent than in walled-off West Berlin.

After Kennedy returned from a long, sober look at the jagged concrete-and-stone-block wall Khrushchev had erected to halt the flood of East Berliners into the West, he stood atop a high podium in front of the city hall and faced more than 1,000,000 persons who had gathered in the huge square.

There he declared, "All free men, wherever they may live, are citizens of Berlin, and, therefore, as a free man, I take pride in the words, '*Ich Bin Ein Berliner!*'"

His German pronunciation was dreadful, but the sentiment he expressed struck his listeners in the heart. The tidal wave of roars was unlike anything he had ever heard before. Many in the vast crowd wept; others were close to hysteria.

After Berlin, Jack, accompanied by Jean Smith and Eunice Shriver, went to Dunganstown, Ireland, for a visit to his ancestoral roots. It was a three-day sentimental journey during which he met and dined with cousins in their modest homes, teased his hosts about the salmon they served (was it caught illegally?), and charmed the multitudes who flocked to see him.

His aides, unable to break the habit of measuring crowd response, told him he could easily have been elected to the Dail, the Irish parliament, or even higher office. After he left, according to Ralph G. Martin, a Dublin newspaper reported that 375 Irish women said they had slept with Kennedy during his visit.

And Cuba Again

"Things just aren't right, said a worried Charles Halleck, the House Republican leader, in September, 1962. "They goddamned well need to do something, but they aren't doing it!"

Khrushchev was in a bind back home. The Russian economy was on a downhill slide, he was lagging behind the U.S. in the missile race, and was being taunted constantly by the Chinese for veering away from Marxist communism. He needed a political shot in the arm, and Halleck, along with many others in Washington, knew it.

What *was* he doing? Intelligence reports filtering into the White House said that the Soviets were beefing up Cuban defenses with dozens of anti-aircraft weapons and thousands of technicians to teach Castro's soldiers to use them. But this, Kennedy said in a statement, was insurance against any attempt on the part of the U.S. to invade the island.

But would he dare go further? Would he place missiles capable of delivering nuclear bombs there? Pentagon analysts told Kennedy they hardly thought he would. Russia had never before placed nuclear weapons beyond its own borders, so why would she start now? they reasoned. At the same time, high government officials noted that the United States had plenty of nuclear-tipped missiles beyond *its* borders pointed at Russia — 60 Thors in Britain, 30 Jupiters in Italy, and another 15 in Turkey. Why shouldn't the aggressive Khrushchev play tit for tat?

Why not, indeed, since after the Vienna summit Khrushchev had sized up President Kennedy as intelligent and reasonable but inexperienced in hard-ball international power politics. If the stakes were high enough, the Soviet leader believed, the American President could be bluffed out of the pot.

Khrushchev misjudged Kennedy badly. He undertook to place missiles capable of delivering nuclear bombs inside Cuba, aimed at the U.S. Had war erupted, Kennedy explained later, 45 percent of the population of the country at the time — some 80,000,000 men, women, and children — would have perished in a few hours.

He called the Russian's bluff.

The crisis began on October 14, 1962, when a U-2 spy plane, photographing the Cuban terrain from twelve miles up, detected at least a half dozen missile sites in various stages of construction. After Kennedy inspected the photos, he telephoned Bobby. "Come here soon as you can," he said. "We're facing great trouble."

For the next thirteen days, the world edged toward the abyss. More U-2 flights showed work being speeded up on the missile bases. Kennedy knew if the United States allowed them to be completed, the power balance between the two countries would be completely altered.

To help him deal with the dilemma, Kennedy called together sixteen high-ranking officials, forming them into an Executive Committee of the National Security Council (EXCOM). The committee met almost nonstop in the Cabinet room, wrestling over the options: Invade Cuba? Wipe out the sites by an air attack? Bomb all the airfields in Cuba?

Bobby, doodling on a pad as he listened to the advice on how and where to launch the air strikes, scribbled a note and passed it to the President:

"I now know how Tojo felt when he was planning Pearl Harbor."

Any of the moves mentioned above by the U.S. would invite certain retaliation. As the days went on, each of the sixteen EXCOM members received evacuation orders in the event of imminent attack: The government would be moved to a secret site outside the capital and they were to rush there the moment word was flashed that missiles were on their way to destroy Washington. The instructions included the chilling order that no wives or children were to be taken.

The Kennedy brothers would go, too. The government had to be maintained. EXCOM members called their wives and, in what had to be the saddest conversations of their lives, asked them to leave the city at once. Some did, taking their children; others refused.

Jackie told her husband she would remain in the White House. Ethel told Bobby she would not leave Hickory Hill.

John Kennedy refused to use force unless absolutely essential. He decided on another course.

On Monday, October 22, he told the nation he had decided to impose a selective naval blockade, barring all ships carrying missile equipment from proceeding closer than 500 miles to Cuba. Starting Wednesday at ten A.M., any vessel running the blockade (or "quarantine," as he termed it) would be stopped and seized.

The Soviet Union gave no intention of heeding. A flotilla of 25 Russian vessels, guarded by submarines, was heading toward the island and there was no halt to construction at the six MRBM missile sites. The U.S., for its part, was gearing up for action: 180 ships were sent by the navy into the Caribbean, and B-52 bombers, loaded with atomic warheads, were ordered on instant alert by the Strategic Air Command. To Bobby, a direct military confrontation seemed inevitable, and the President, deep in gloom, agreed.

On Wednesday the world held its breath as the 25 Soviet ships streamed toward the quarantine zone. John Kennedy was in the Oval Office much of the day, listening to reports from EXCOM and planning strategy. Once, says Dave Powers, he took time out to help Caroline and Jackie carve some Halloween pumpkins.

On Thursday, 16 vessels stopped before the line, swung around, and sailed back. The others halted in mid-ocean, dropping anchor, and remained, but the crisis was far from over. New aerial photographs clearly showed that work on the missile bases had been stepped up.

"Doom was in the air," said Pierre Salinger as the members of EXCOM continued their round-the-clock sessions in the Cabinet room. However, the city of Washington was taking the confrontation in stride. There was no evidence of tension anywhere. The usual traffic flowed past the White House along Pennsylvania Avenue, and only a trickle of pedestrians walked past the mansion, barely glancing at it. The only signs of the momentous drama being played out were the limousines that came and went all day along, discharging passengers at the west wing.

On Friday, a glimmer of hope pierced the gloom. - A conciliatory message came from Khrushchev: if the U.S. pledged not to invade Cuba, the U.S.S.R. would remove its missiles. But next day, a second, much harsher letter arrived, escalating the Kremlin's demands. The U.S., it said, must also remove its missiles from Turkey.

"It was Black Saturday," remarked George Ball, Undersecretary of State.

Kennedy was furious at the new message, which put him in a catch-22 position. If he yielded, he would appear weak; if he turned the proposal down, he might trigger a war. To clear his mind and vent his rage, he strode around the President's Park.

New Intelligence photographs had come in. By the middle of the following week, experts estimated, the sites would be completed and ready for action. About 30 nuclear missiles had been counted on the island, plus about 20 jet bombers capable of delivering atomic bombs. The U.S. was ready with its warships and and B-52 bombers.

The abyss was yawning.

Black Saturday wore on. In the afternoon, an idea occurred to Bobby Kennedy. Ignore the tough second letter, he suggested, and send Khrushchev a reply to the more conciliatory first message. At eight P.M. the answer went out: President Kennedy accepted the First Secretary's terms — no invasion in return for removal of the missiles and destruction of the sites.

Nobody knew how the Soviet premier would react. Robert S. McNamara looked at the brilliantly descending sun at twilight and said, "I wonder how many more sunsets I will see."

On Sunday morning, October 28, Khrushchev's answer came: "The Soviet government has given a new order to dismantle the arms which you described as offensive, and to crate them and return them to the Soviet Union."

That evening, Jack and Bobby indulged in some gallows humor. In a reference to Abraham Lincoln, assassinated in Ford's Theatre five days after Robert E. Lee surrendered and the Civil War crisis was resolved, Jack said, "Maybe this is the night I should go to the theater."

Bobby replied, "If you go, I want to go with you."

Chapter Nine

Wars At Home

On the domestic front: The pride of all Americans, and especially that of its young, competitive leader, was deeply wounded on April 12, 1961, when the twenty-seven-year-old Russian cosmonaut, Yuri A. Gagarin, became the first man to travel into space. The Soviet accomplishment could cost Kennedy the Presidency in 1964, his aides grumbled. Kennedy acted promptly. He announced a bold program to put a man on the moon, and return him safely, in the next decade.

In April, 1962, Kennedy took on the head of United States Steel, accusing Roger Blough of bad faith in raising costs after participating in conferences to hold down steelworkers' wages, with the underlying assumption that the company would hold the line on prices. When other companies joined in the increase, the outraged President clashed head-on with the steel industry, and won.

The civil rights issue had exploded four months after he took office and was to fester throughout his administration. In May, 1961, the Freedom Riders rode through Southern states in an attempt to integrate facilities in bus terminals closed to blacks. In October, federal troops and U.S. marshals put down rioting that wrecked the campus of the University of Mississippi when a black student sought admission.

In June, 1963, the administration again used the National Guard to force the University of Alabama to enroll two black students.

Space And Steel

After the Soviets stunned and humiliated the U.S. by hurling man's first artificial satellite into space on October 4, 1957, Sherman Adams, Ike's chief assistant, said the nation wasn't interested in an "outer space basketball game." The remark, for which he later apologized, was intended to undercut efforts to engage in a space race with Russia.

It didn't work. The launching of *Sputnik I*, a 184-pound globe 2 feet in diameter, started an intense rivalry that began in the last years of Ike's term and intensified in the Kennedy years. Given John Kennedy's competitive nature, it was hardly surprising that he took the Soviet challenge personally. In no mood to accept another defeat so soon after the Bay of Pigs, albeit of a different kind, at the hands of communists, he went before Congress on May 25, 1961, to deliver a special, second State of the Union address. He roused the nation, and most of the legislators, with a stirring speech.

He was aware, he said, that he was asking an incredible sum (for those days, and even now) — about $9,000,000,000 — for space exploration, but the challenge to national pride was urgent and the eventual benefits enormous.

"I believe," he told Congress, "that this nation should commit itself to achieving the goal, before this decade is out, of landing a man on the moon and returning him safely to earth."

He received an ovation — and the money.

Before he had decided to commit himself to the space adventure, Kennedy had many misgivings about the cost. Wistfully he asked a group of prominent scientists he had called together to discuss the subject: "Can't you fellows invent some other race here on earth. . . ?"

In the late afternoon of April 10, 1962, balding, bespectacled Roger Blough, board chairman of the United States Steel Corporation, stunned and infuriated Kennedy with an unexpected announcement. Meeting in the Oval Office, Blough informed the President that Big Steel would increase its prices by $6 a ton. Even as they spoke, Blough said, a four-page press release was being distributed to all news media, announcing the new scales.

It was the opening scene in an economic drama that pitted J.F.K. against the most powerful leaders of the business community.

Only four days before, negotiations between the United Steel Workers of America and the industry had concluded with a moderate increase in wages. The administration had urged both sides to accept a non-inflationary pact: a small wage increase, no rise in prices. The union accepted, and while there had been no formal agreement with the steel companies, the administration had assumed an understanding had been reached that prices would remain stable.

Kennedy viewed the signing of the contract as a major victory. If steel held the line, so would other industries; if the steel union made only moderate demands, so would labor everywhere. The menace of inflation, which would seriously jeopardize the country's economy, would be dampened.

Coldly, Kennedy said to Blough: "I think you have made a terrible mistake."

He called in Arthur Goldberg, then Secretary of Labor, who angrily told Blough the increases would not only hurt the nation but shred the administration's credibility in the eyes of all labor unions.

After Blough left, Kennedy, feeling he had been blind-sided by Big Steel, fumed at the "pricks" and "bastards" in the industry.

"My father always told me that all businessmen were sons-of-bitches," he said, "but I never believed it until now."

"This is war!" the President said.

The following day, Bethlehem Steel had upped its prices within hours, four other major producers — Republic Steel, Jones & Laughlin, Youngstown and Wheeling — joined the move. From Kaiser, Colorado Fuel & Iron, and Inland Steel came word that the situation was under study.

Kennedy's opening assault came at three-thirty P.M. that day at a televised press conference. Terming the increase "a wholly unjustifiable and

247

irresponsible defiance of the public interest," he pointed out that if the industry followed Big Steel's lead, "it would increase the costs of homes, autos, appliances, and most other items for every American family. It would increase the cost of machinery and tools to every American businessman and farmer. It would seriously handicap our efforts to prevent an inflationary spiral from eating up the pensions of our older citizens, and our new gains in purchasing power. It would also increase the cost of national defense by $1 billion," he said, "make it tougher for American goods to compete in foreign markets and handicap efforts to induce other industries and unions to adopt responsible price and wage policies."

He concluded with this bitter castigation: "Some time ago I asked each American to consider what he would do for his country, and I asked the steel companies. In the last twenty-four hours, we had their answer."

All agencies of the government were mobilized to fight the war.

Bobby announced that his department had already convened a grand jury to look into the possibility that the major steel producers were violating criminal laws against price-fixing. Already, he said, subpoenas had been slapped on a number of top officials.

The Department of Defense, which purchased vast quantities of steel each year, said it would no longer buy any from the firms that had raised prices. To prove it meant it, the department announced that the Lukens Steel Company, which had not joined the others, would get a $5,000,000 contract for a special armor plate for Polaris-missile submarines.

The Federal Trade Commission began digging into the business backgrounds of the offending firms, searching for violations of regulations. If any were found, the F.T.C. said, swift action would follow.

A jawboning drive by telephone was hastily organized. J.F.K. phoned Edgar Kaiser, president of Kaiser Steel; Undersecretary of the Treasury Henry Fowler called the president of Inland Steel; Bobby Kennedy, Robert McNamara, and Arthur Goldberg put through calls to other powerful men in the industry. Their message: Price increases are bad for the country. Rescind them or else . . .

Administration officials were not reticent about spelling out the "or else." Big Steel, already too big, might be fragmented into a number of little steel units. Laws might be sought setting limits on all steel prices and adding sharper teeth to existing antitrust laws.

The first sign that the industry might yield came at ten-fifteen on the morning of April 13. Inland Steel said that after reviewing the situation, price increases would not be in the national interest. A few hours later, Kaiser joined Inland. In mid-afternoon, Bethlehem Steel capitulated, and at six P.M. Big Steel threw in the towel.

Kennedy won the "war" in three days.⁵

Steel-company executives ordered special buttons made, which they pinned to their jackets and wore in their offices during the crisis. The buttons, in large letters, read: "S.O.B."

Civil Rights

Less than a month after Gagarin's flight, thirteen young blacks and whites made their own historic journey on a bus in America. These "Freedom Riders," soon joined by others, were bloodied by mobs wielding baseball bats, tire chains, black jacks, and sticks. Near Anniston, Alabama, a fire bomb destroyed their bus, but they got another one and continued on.

In Birmingham, they were rushed by a gang of Ku Klux Klansmen and beaten for ten minutes; three were injured so seriously that they were hospitalized. Police, who knew the bus was en route and that violence would surely erupt, were nowhere about.

Eugene "Bull" Connor, the city's burly police commissioner, had an explanation: It was Mother's Day and he had told many of his men to take the day off. He was left with only a skeleton force of, presumably, motherless cops to keep the peace in the city.

In Montgomery, Alabama, Dr. Martin Luther King, Jr., of the Southern Christian Leadership

Conference, prepared to address a rally of 1,500 blacks jammed into that city's First Baptist Church to cheer on the riders. As he entered the church, King saw a huge crowd of hostile whites gathering in the park not far from the church.

Trouble was brewing.

A force of 100 federal marshals, armed with police truncheons and tear-gas grenades, was rushed to the scene by Byron White, then Deputy Attorney General. They arrived just in time. The crowd in the park surged forward to attack the church. In hand-to-hand combat, the marshals defended the church and themselves with tear gas and nightsticks, ducking, if they could, the rocks hurled at them.

Despite the tightly closed windows, tear gas seeped into the church. As the battle raged outside, the barricaded blacks, perspiring in the unusual heat, prayed and sang. Sensing that many were on the verge of panic, Dr. King sang with them and spoke reassuringly from the pulpit. But inwardly, he was far from reassured himself.

From the church office in the basement, Dr. King telephoned Bobby in Washington.

"He was concerned about whether he was going to live and whether his people were going to live," Bobby said later. "He kept getting these reports that the crowds were moving in and that they were going to burn the church down and shoot the Negroes as they ran out of the church.

"I said that our people were down there and that as long as he was in the church, he might say a prayer for us. He didn't think that was very humorous."

Dr. King told Bobby angrily that the administration had betrayed him and his people by not providing enough protection. "Now, Reverend," Bobby replied, "don't tell me that. You know just as well as I do that if it hadn't been for the United States marshals you'd be as dead as Kelsey's nuts right now."

There was a dead silence on the line. The Atlanta-born King hadn't the vaguest notion who Kelsey was, but he got the drift.

Outside the church, the Alabama National Guard and state troopers arrived and, with the marshals, drove back the mob. Between five and six A.M. the 1,500 besieged blacks left and, escorted by Guardsmen, returned to their homes.

When the Kennedy brothers finally heard that the church had been evacuated without loss of life, they toasted each other with a glass of beer.

The civil-rights struggle continued unabated. A fifteen-hour battle raged on the campus of "Ole Miss," the University of Mississippi in Oxford, when a black man sought admission for the first time since the school was founded in 1844. Two persons were killed, hundreds injured, hundreds more jailed, and much of the campus was wrecked before quiet was restored and James H. Meredith was finally enrolled.

Murder and violence flared in many cities, some in the North, but most in the Deep South. Bombs wrecked the homes of black leaders. Four girls were killed when a church was dynamited in

Birmingham. In Florida, four black men, including a dentist, were kidnapped by Ku Klux Klansmen and set afire after being beaten unconscious; the sheriff and his deputies arrived just in time to save their lives.

Birmingham was the scene of the worst series of incidents. Television brought into the nation's homes horrifying scenes of police dogs snapping at black women, high-pressure water hoses sweeping blacks down the streets like matchsticks, and black businesses put to the torch. There was open warfare on the streets as furious blacks, armed with knives, bricks, and stones, attacked Bull Connor's cops. Finally, after hundreds of state troopers rushed in, the violence abated.

Barely had order been restored when a new confrontation began shaping up in Tuscaloosa, to the southwest. Two blacks were attempting to enroll in the University of Alabama — over Governor George Wallace's body, planted firmly in front of the door to the registration building. A federal court had decreed that the university had to take them, and Assistant Attorney General Nicholas Katzenbach came down to see that the law was upheld.

Tuscaloosa was tense as hundreds of riot-trained troops were poised to move in if the blacks were barred and violence broke out. But after a dramatic *High Noon*-type face-off, Wallace caved in and the blacks were admitted.

In Washington, Kennedy felt the moment had finally come to put the power and prestige of his administration behind the civil-rights revolution.

"There comes a time," he told aides, "when a man must take a stand." With Ted Sorensen, he began drafting a speech that he said could cost him re-election in 1964.

It has been called the second Emancipation Proclamation.

Martin Luther King, Jr., had used that phrase when he met Kennedy at a Los Angeles rally just before the nominating convention in 1960. King's words, as they shook hands, were: "You know, we need a civil-rights bill for the disadvantaged. A real civil-rights bill. A sort of second Emancipation Proclamation."

The parallel is striking. On January 1, 1863, Abraham Lincoln formally issued the historic edict that declared the slaves in the rebellious states to be "forever free."

A century later, on June 11, 1963, just hours after Wallace capitulated, Kennedy went before the microphones. In urgent, impassioned tones he delivered the last of the three great speeches of his administration: He said, in part:

Today we are committed to a worldwide struggle to promote and protect the rights of all who wish to be free. And when Americans are sent to Vietnam or West Berlin, we do not ask for whites only. It ought to be possible, therefore, for American students of any color to attend any public institution they select without having to be backed up by troops.

It ought to be possible for American consumers of any color to receive equal service in places of public accommodation, such as hotels and restaurants and theaters and retail stores, without being forced to resort to demonstrations in the street, and it ought to be possible for American citizens of any color to register and to vote in a free election without interference or fear of reprisal.

It ought to be possible, in short, for every American to enjoy the privileges of being American without regard to his race or his color. In short, every American ought to have the right to be treated as he would wish to be treated as one would wish his children to be treated. But this is not the case.

The Negro baby born in America today, regardless of the section of the nation in which he is born, has about one-half as much chance of completing a high school as a white baby born in the same place on the same day, one-third as much chance of completing college, one-third as much chance of becoming a professional man, twice as much chance of becoming unemployed, about one-seventh as much chance of earning $10,000 a year, a life expectancy which is seven years shorter, and the prospects of earning only half as much. . . .

We are confronted primarily with a moral issue. It is as old as the Scriptures and is as clear as the American Constitution.

The heart of the question is whether all Americans are to be afforded equal rights and equal opportunities, whether we are going to treat our fellow Americans as we want to be treated. If an American, because his skin is dark, cannot eat lunch in a restaurant open to the public, if he cannot send his children to the best public school available, if he cannot vote for the public officials who represent him, if, in short, he cannot enjoy the full and free life which all of us want, then who among us would be content to have the color of his skin changed and stand in his place? Who among us would then be content with the counsels of patience and delay?

One hundred years of delay have passed since President Lincoln freed the slaves, yet their heirs, their grandsons, are not fully free. They are not yet freed from the bonds of injustice. They are not yet freed from social and economic oppression. And this nation, for all its hopes and all its boasts, will not be fully free until all its citizens are free. . . .

We face, therefore, a moral crisis as a country and as a people. It cannot be met by repressive police action. It cannot be left to increased demonstrations in the streets. It cannot be quieted by token moves or talk. It is a time to act in Congress, in your state and local legislative body and, above all, in all of our daily lives.

It was a magnificent speech, but there were miles to go before anybody slept.

Several hours after Kennedy spoke, a black man was driving home after attending a rally in a church in Jackson, Mississippi. He parked his car and walked to the door. As he reached it, a shot rang out.

Medgar Evers, field secretary for the National Association for the Advancement of Colored People in Mississippi, and leader in the national civil-rights revolution, fell to the ground, slain by a gunman lurking in the shadows.

Kennedy's speech, author Jim Bishop said later, was "a bolder commitment than Abraham Lincoln had uttered in January, 1963." Its call for action was followed eight days later by a special message urging Congress to remain in session until a comprehensive civil-rights law was passed. Accompanying the message, which warned that continuing frustration would inevitably result in more, and worse, violence, was the draft of a bill calling for an end to discrimination in jobs and public accommodations and a speed-up of school desegration and voting rights.

But Congress did not heed. The bill was bottled up in committee and never reached the floor of either house. John Kennedy did not live to see his bill enacted, but the following year, with President Lyndon Johnson foursquare behind it, the civil-rights Act of 1964 was passed and signed into law on July 2.

The revolution still had far to go, but much progress had been made during Kennedy's administration. Schlesinger recalls that J.F.K. believed that one individual was most responsible for the forward steps in the movement — the bald, bespectacled commissioner of public safety in Alabama, Bull Connor.

Connor was the last person anybody would pick, but Kennedy explained that the TV shots of Connor's snarling dogs and high-powered hoses unleashed against men, women, and children shook the country and, at long last, "awakened the American conscience."

The Days Narrow Down

In November, 1963, Kennedy, reading the Texas newspapers, decided that something had to be done to heal the schism there between two opposing factions of the Democratic Party, one headed by Governor John Bo Connally, Jr., the other by Senator Ralph W. Yarborough.

The battling was not new. Texas-style politics was as chaotic as in Massachusetts, and could be just as great a risk for candidates. For years the conservative wing of the party, representing the oil and business interests, had clashed with the liberal group, heirs to the Populist movement of the 1930s. Connally headed the conservative group, Yarborough the liberal-leftist axis. The battle, Kennedy learned, had grown increasingly rancorous and was threatening to split the party wide open.

Texas has 24 electoral votes; only California, New York, Pennsylvania, and Ohio had more. With 1964 not far off, Kennedy would not take any chances with almost 10 percent of the Electoral College votes he would need for reelection. He decided to go to Texas to heal the rift.

It was not a journey he would willingly undertake. "I hate like hell to make the trip and get into a pissing match," he told his friend George Smathers.

His schedule called for speeches in San Antonio and Houston on November 21, then in Fort Worth and Dallas the next day. He asked Jackie to accompany him, telling her to take along some smashing clothes. "Show these rich Texas broads what it's like to be well dressed," he said.

Other high-ranking officials were also unenthusiastic about the trip.

United Nations Ambassador Adlai Stevenson called the White House and expressed deep reservations. An undercurrent of hatred was seething in Dallas, he said, recalling that on October 24 hostile crowds had booed and spat upon him.

Even before the Stevenson incident, Jack had been warned by Senator J. William Fulbright to avoid Dallas because it was "a very dangerous place." He told the President, "I wouldn't go there. Don't you go."

In mid-November, Ted Kennedy, then the junior senator from Massachusetts, flew to New York to address a convention of the A.F.L.-C.I.O. in a midtown hotel. When his car stopped for a traffic light, a young woman ran up, pointed a camera through the window, and pressed the shutter. A policeman, who had been unable to stop her, commented as the senator's car moved off, "She might well have been an assassin."

Bobby heard all the warnings and was deeply concerned. On November 20, the evening before Jack was to leave for Texas, he and Ramsey Clark, then an Assistant Attorney General, discussed the journey at the annual White House reception for Justice Department lawyers and staff members. "I don't want him to go," Bobby told Clark.

The next morning John and Jackie Kennedy boarded Air Force One at Andrews Air Force Base in Maryland. They sat in the Presidential compartment just aft of the wings, as Colonel James Swindal, the command pilot, lifted the big blue-and-white Boeing 707 off the ground, bound for Texas.

Sources and Acknowledgments

Many of the anecdotes and incidents in this book came from the authors' Kennedy files, accumulated over a quarter-century of reporting on the family. Talks over the years with Edward M. Kennedy, Joan Kennedy, Rose Kennedy, and other family members were drawn upon. New interviews with numerous persons whose lives touched those of the Kennedys provided additional material. Invaluable source material were the hundreds of Oral Histories at the John F. Kennedy Library at Columbia Point, Boston. The extensive archives and manuscript collections there — in particular, the personal papers of John F. Kennedy — were also prime sources. The assistance of the library's archival staff, above and far beyond the call of duty, is herewith gratefully acknowledged.

Also consulted were newspaper and magazine files, in particular those of *The New York Times, Washington Post, New York Herald-Tribune* (now defunct), *Los Angeles Times, Boston Globe,* and *Springfield Union. The Ladies' Home Journal, McCall's, Look* and *Life* were also consulted. Books that proved particulary helpful were the following:

Baker, Bobby. *Wheeling and Dealing: Confessions of a Capitol Hill Operator.* New York: W. W. Norton & Co., 1978.

Bishop, Jim. *The Days of Martin Luther King, Jr.* New York: G. P. Putnam's Sons, 1971.

Bradlee, Benjamin C. *Conversations with Kennedy.* New York: W. W. Norton & Co., 1975.

Burner, David, and Thomas R. West. *The Torch Is Passed: The Kennedy Brothers and American Liberalism.* New York: Atheneum, 1984.

Cameron, Gail. *Rose.* New York: G. P. Putnam's Sons, 1971.

Cate, Curtis. *The Ides of August: The Berlin Crisis, 1961.* New York: M. Evans and Company, Inc., 1978.

Dallas, Rita. *The Kennedy Case.* G. P. Putnam's Sons, 1971.

David, Lester. *Ted Kennedy: Triumphs and Tragedies.* New York: Grosset & Dunlap, 1971.

——— *Ethel: The Story of Mrs. Robert F. Kennedy.* New York and Cleveland: The World Publishing Company, 1971.

——— *Joan: The Reluctant Kennedy.* New York, Funk & Wagnalls, 1974.

Devine, Robert A., ed. *Cuban Missile Crisis,* Chicago: Quadrangle Books, 1971.

Dineen, Joseph F. *The Kennedy Family.* Boston, Toronto: Little, Brown & Co., 1959.

Garrow, David J. *Martin Luther King, Jr., and the Southern Christian Leadership Conference.* New York: William Morrow and Company, Inc., 1986.

Gelb Norman. *The Berlin Wall: Kennedy, Khrushchev, and a Showdown in the Heart of Europe.* New York: Times Books, 1986.

Kelley, Kitty. *Jackie Oh!* Secaucus, N.J.: Lyle Stuart, 1978.

Kennedy, Rose Fitzgerald. *Times to Remember.* Garden City, N. Y.: Doubleday & Co., 1974.

King, Coretta Scott. *My Life with Martin Luther King, Jr.* New York, Chicago, San Francisco: Holt, Rinehart and Winston, 1969.

Krock, Arthur. *Memoirs: Sixty Years on the Firing Line.* New York: Funk & Wagnalls, 1968.

Lasky, Victor. *JFK: The Man and the Myth.* New York: Macmillan, 1963.

Lawford, Patricia, ed. *That Shining Hour.* Privately published.

Lincoln, Evelyn. *My Twelve Years with John F. Kennedy.* New York: David McKay Co., 1965.

Manchester, William. *The Glory and the Dream.* Boston, Toronto: Little, Brown & Co., 1973–74.

Martin, Ralph G. *A Hero for Our Time: An Intimate Story of the Kennedy Years.* New York: Macmillan, 1983.

O'Donnell, Kenneth P., and David F. Powers. *Johnny We Hardly Knew Ye.* Boston, Toronto: Little, Brown & Co., 1970–72.

Parmet, Herbert S. *Jack: The Struggles of John Kennedy.* Garden City, N.Y.: The Dial Press, 1980.

———— *JFK. The Presidency of John F. Kennedy.* Garden City, N.Y.: Doubleday & Co., 1966.

Salinger, Pierre. *With Kennedy.* Garden City, N.Y.: Doubleday and Co., 1966.

Schlesinger, Arthur M., Jr. *A Thousand Days: John F. Kennedy in the White House.* Boston: Houghton Mifflin Co.; Cambridge: The Riverside Press, 1965.

Sharnik, John. *Inside the Cold War: An Oral History.* New York: Arbor House, 1987.

Sidey, Hugh. *John F. Kennedy: A Reporter's Inside Story.* New York: Atheneum, 1963.

Smith, Marie. *Entertaining in the White House.* New York: McFadden Bartell Corp., 1970.

Sorensen, Theodore C. *Kennedy.* New York: Bantam, 1966.

———— *The Kennedy Legacy: A Peaceful Revolution for the Seventies.* New York: Macmillan, 1969.

West, J. B. *Upstairs at the White House.* New York: Coward, McCann & Geoghegan, 1973.

Wofford, Harris. *Of Kennedys and Kings.* New York: Farrar, Straus & Giroux, 1980.

Wyden, Peter. *Bay of Pigs: The Untold Story.* New York: Simon & Shuster, 1979.

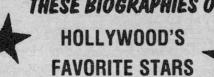

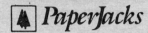

GET IN SHAPE

WITH HELP FROM

▲ PaperJacks

DIET AND HEALTH BOOKS

____ **EARL MINDELL'S PILL BIBLE**
The complete nutritional guide for
everyone who takes pills   7701-08695/$4.50
                                          CDN/$5.50

____ **ENERGISTICS** — Phyllis Paulette
Twelve steps to vitality, health,
and well being   7701-0568-8/$3.95

____ **FOOD SENSITIVITY DIET** — Doug. A.
Kaufmann — Follow the simple program that has
helped thousands lose weight and lead
happier, healthier lives.   7701-0471-1/$3.95

____ **THAT FIRST BITE** — Karen Rose
Journal of a compulsive overeater.
                                  7701-0647-1/$3.95

Available at your local bookstore or return this coupon to:

FREE!!
BOOKS BY MAIL
CATALOGUE

BOOKS BY MAIL will share with you our current bestselling books as well as hard to find specialty titles in areas that will match your interests. You will be updated on what's new in books at no cost to you. Just fill in the coupon below and discover the convenience of having books delivered to your home.

PLEASE ADD $1.00 TO COVER THE COST OF POSTAGE & HANDLING.

BOOKS BY MAIL

320 Steelcase Road E.,
Markham, Ontario L3R 2M1

IN THE U.S. -
210 5th Ave., 7th Floor
New York, N.Y., 10010

Please send Books By Mail catalogue to:

Name _____
(please print)

Address _____

City _____

Prov./State _____ P.C./Zip _____

(BBM1)